Application Development with PowerBuilder

Application Development with PowerBuilder

James Hobuss

A Wiley–QED Publication

John Wiley & Sons, Inc.

New York • Chichester • Brisbane • Toronto • Singapore

Publisher: K. Schowalter
Editor: Ed Kerr
Managing Editor: Mark Hayden
Editorial Production & Design: Publishers' Design and Production Services, Inc.

Designations used by companies to distinguish their products are often claimed as trademarks. In all instances where John Wiley & Sons, Inc. is aware of a claim, the product names appear in initial capital or all capital letters. Readers, however, should contact the appropriate companies for more complete information regarding trademarks and registration.

This text is printed on acid-free paper.

This publication is designed to provide accurate and authoritative information in regard to the subject matter covered. It is sold with the understanding that the publisher is not engaged in rendering legal, accounting, or other professional services. If legal advice or other expert assistance is required, the services of a competent professional person should be sought.

Library of Congress Cataloging-in-Publication Data

Hobuss, James J., 1955–
    Application development with PowerBuilder / James Hobuss.
      p. cm.
    "A Wiley/QED publication."
    Includes index.
    ISBN 0-471-06067-4 (paper)
    1. Application software. 2. PowerBuilder. I. Title.
QA76.76.A65H63   1994
005.265—dc20   94-12668
                                                      CIP

Printed in the United States of America

10 9 8 7 6 5 4 3 2 1

Dedication

Once again, and always, to my wife, Robin, for her unending support, encouragement, and love, which creates limitless boundaries and a world as close to nirvana as this beating heart will ever know. To Colleen Lawrence, for her help in finalizing the preparation of this manuscript and her dedication to help build my dream. To Michael Charles Lee, for his help and friendship which has meant so much over the years. To Rich Sutherland, for introducing me to PowerBuilder and his persistence that this was a tool I must look at. To Steve Karlen and Gary Bilodeau, for their help and sharing of PowerBuilder expertise.

Contents

Preface

When this project began, there were no books on the market for PowerBuilder. In fact, Powersoft Corp. knew of no books "in the works." This was quite surprising, given the popularity of the tool and the huge success of the product. By the time you read these words, however, there will be at least two (and possibly more) books available on PowerBuilder.

I hope, you will purchase this one. I'll give you some reasons why:

1) As an application developer with almost twenty years of experience in the industry, I learned a few things along the way. First, I learned the 80/20 rule. This rule states that 80 percent of the time you will use 20 percent of a product's features and capabilities. A complementary paradigm is that at no time will you ever use 100 percent of the features and capabilities of any software product. Given this to be true (if you disagree with me, I'd love to hear from you and discuss it), I have made no attempt to write a reference book on PowerBuilder. Such a book would be too exhaustive to write, too expensive to produce, and you would never want to buy it. It would probably be out of date by the time it hit the shelves, due to the time it would take to write. Rather, I have developed the book with a keen determination to make it as useful as possible for learning about the more commonly used

features of PowerBuilder. Although I have not covered 100 percent of the product features in this book, I believe I have given ample attention to the features used to develop applications.

2) As President of HCS, Inc. since spring 1991, making it my business to deliver high-quality instructor-led training classes, I believe I know how to break down complex subject matter into understandable parcels. Make no mistake about it, once you scratch through the first layers of PowerBuilder, you will quickly discover it is a complex product. This is where my experience in developing and presenting high-technology training courses is valuable. This book has broken down even the most complex components of the product into easily understood pieces.

3) There are nearly 300 screen images in the book. There are two reasons for this large number. First, they can (and should) be used as navigation points for you when using the product and attempting to reference a topic in the book. Second, they allow you to orient yourself to the product much more quickly than reading pages and pages of text.

If you are already an application developer using PowerBuilder, you will receive value from this book by the abundant examples that are provided illustrating so many of the product features. If you are a programmer just now (or soon) beginning to use Power-Builder, the purchase of this book is a wise decision—it will pay for itself many times over in minimizing the learning curve associated with a product such as this. You will be productive sooner after reading this book.

If you don't buy this book now, don't worry. Either this book (or another copy of the same title) may be here when you come back to purchase it later. But you shouldn't wait too long to come back, as the next person to buy this book is just now walking through the door.

This book is designed to teach programmers (and people interested in programming) who are familiar with PCs and Microsoft Windows how to use PowerBuilder by Powersoft Inc. PowerBuilder is a graphical application builder toolset that comes complete with a GUI interface painter, application management tools, proprietary programming language, and several DBMS interfaces, not to mention a DBMS of its own.

Specifically, this book covers the following:

- Features and capabilities of the PowerBuilder product
- Key terms and general knowledge required to develop a graphical user interface application in PowerBuilder
- The PowerBuilder application development environment
- Steps required to create a PowerBuilder Application
- Management and maintenance of PowerBuilder Preferences
- Database administration tasks using the PowerBuilder Database Painter
- Using the PowerBuilder Application Painter
- Creation of windows and dialogues using the PowerBuilder Window Painter
- Writing PowerBuilder applications using PowerScript and covering the following language elements:
  - General language elements
  - Datatypes
  - Variable declaration
  - Using attributes
  - Using functions
  - Decision coding
  - Looping
  - Basic PowerBuilder functions
  - Global or user functions
- Using SQL with PowerScript
- Application debugging techniques
- Description and use of PowerBuilder DataWindows
- Packaging PowerBuilder applications into *.exe files for distribution

Overview of the Book Organization

It is recommended that the reader take a basic Microsoft Windows training course (or have equivalent work experience) before attempting to develop a PowerBuilder application to get full value from reading this book. Also, an introductory level understanding of graphical user interface (GUI) concepts and design is recommended. Knowledge and experience with Structured Query

Language (SQL), specifically using one of the DBMSs that interface with PowerBuilder, is desired but not required.

Given the foregoing, the following is a chapter-by-chapter itemization of the topics.

Chapter 1—PowerBuilder Product Overview

Introduction to Powersoft Corp.
Company goals, product features, technical support
PowerBuilder hardware/software requirements
Third-party DBMS product support
Current version information
Introduction to the components of the PowerBuilder Application development environment

Chapter 2—PowerBuilder Terminology

Definition of a control or object
Window controls and their components
Other controls placed on windows
Control attributes
Menus
Parent/child relationships—different kinds of windows
Object-oriented concepts—inheritance, polymorphism, encapsulation
Event-driven applications
Client/server

Chapter 3—The PowerBuilder Environment

The basics of the PowerBuilder development environment
The Power Panel with functions of each icon
The different PowerBuilder files and their interrelationships
The basic steps in creating an application

Chapter 4—PowerBuilder Preferences

Definition of a Preference in PowerBuilder
Defining Preferences in PowerBuilder
Setting PowerBuilder Application Painter Preferences
Setting PowerBuilder Window Painter Preferences
Setting PowerBuilder Menu Painter Preferences
Setting PowerBuilder DataWindow Painter Preferences
Setting PowerBuilder Database Painter Preferences
Setting PowerBuilder Library Painter Preferences
Setting PowerBuilder Debug Painter Preferences
Setting PowerBuilder Preferences

Chapter 5—PowerBuilder Application Painter

Adding/changing PowerBuilder Application library
Setting up application library search path
Setting up application text default fonts, style, size, and colors
Selecting an icon for the application
Identifying application-level events or functions

Chapter 6—PowerBuilder Database Painter

The capabilities of the PowerBuilder Database Painter
Creating tables with the PowerBuilder Database Painter
Modifying tables with the PowerBuilder Database Painter
Definition of PowerBuilder Database Extended Attributes
Creating indexes with the PowerBuilder Database Painter
Dropping tables, indexes, views with the PowerBuilder Database Painter
The content and structure of the PowerBuilder system tables
Using the PowerBuilder Data Manipulation Tool

Chapter 7—PowerBuilder Window Painter

Entering the PowerBuilder Window Painter
Creating PowerBuilder Windows
Creating all major PowerBuilder controls
Managing all major attributes for each PowerBuilder control
Other features of the PowerBuilder Window Painter

Chapter 8—PowerBuilder Menu Painter

Creating a menu bar for a window with the PowerBuilder
Menu Painter
Creating menu options for menu bar items with the Power-
Builder Menu Painter
Assigning scripts for menu selections with the PowerBuilder
Menu Painter

Chapter 9—PowerBuilder PowerScript

Definition of PowerScript
Using the PowerScript Painter
PowerScript language elements
Operators and expressions
Variable scope
Datatypes
Variable declaration
Changing control attributes
Using PowerBuilder functions
Decision making in PowerScript
Looping in PowerScript

Chapter 10—Debugging under PowerBuilder

Adding/Editing stops in a debug session
Displaying or modifying variables

PowerBuilder Product Overview

This chapter mainly describes PowerBuilder and its hardware and software requirements. You will learn about Powersoft, Inc., its company goals, its products, and how to communicate with technical support—including third-party DBMS product support.

You will learn about the components of the PowerBuilder application development environment, PowerBuilder product features, what you can do with PowerBuilder, and what PowerBuilder can do for you.

POWERSOFT, INC.

PowerBuilder is written and distributed by Powersoft, Incorporated.

Powersoft Corporation
70 Blanchard Road
Burlington MA 01803
(617) 229-2200, (800) 395-3595
Fax: (617) 273-2540

Technical Support: (800) 937-7693
Bulletin Board: (617) 229-9735

Powersoft BBS: (617) 229-9735
Connection Parameters: 8 Databits, No Parity, 1 Stopbit,
Speeds up to 9,600 bps

Faxback Service: (617) 238-6800
On Compuserve: Go POWERSOFT

PowerSoft, Inc. was created in 1974 by Mitchell Kertzman, and originally called Computer Solutions. PowerBuilder development began in 1988, with product introduction in 1991. PowerBuilder is used by a continuously growing install base, contributing to rapid market expansion for leading-edge client/server relational database application building products.

POWERBUILDER REQUIREMENTS

Current Version

3.0B—1993

Minimum Workstation Configuration

386SX, 386DX, or 486 CPU

Minimum 4 Megabytes of RAM

PC-DOS or MS-DOS operating system, version 3.3 or better

Microsoft Windows, version 3.0 or better

Ten (10) Megabytes of hard disk space for PowerBuilder system files, database space, applications, and MicroSoft Windows

EGA, VGA, XVGA, XGA, or 8514A display

Database Management System Interfaces Available

Microsoft/SYBASE SQLServer

Oracle Corporation ORACLE Server

IBM Database Manager or DB2/2 (requires third party database gateway)

Hewlett Packard ALLBASE/SQL

Gupta Technologies SQLBase

XDB Systems XDB

Informix Software INFORMIX

Other interfaces available or planned

Network Support

All networks supported by the installed DBMS vendor

AUTOEXEC.BAT Modifications

```
PATH=...;C:\PB;<DBMS Directory Path>
<Set variables required for DBMS operation>
```

CONFIG.SYS Modifications

```
SHELL=C:\COMMAND.COM /P/E:2048
FILES=245
```

POWERBUILDER: WHAT IS IT?

PowerBuilder is a suite of tools presented in a graphical environment, which can be used to develop object-oriented, graphical user interface (GUI) applications in a client/server environment.

What Does That Mean?

PowerBuilder runs under Microsoft Windows and allows for the creation of applications that also run under Microsoft Windows. These applications can have the same look and feel as any other application program running under Windows, and the user will interact with an application built under PowerBuilder in the same way as with any other Windows program. Data is collected and presented in windows using common graphical user objects, or controls, such as entry fields, radio buttons, list boxes, push-buttons, and the like.

The creation of GUI applications formerly required extensive, detailed, low-level coding in a language such as C. PowerBuilder is an easy-to-use, graphical environment that allows users to "paint" their application, and pull applications together with a simple but powerful script language. PowerBuilder employs the power of object orientation to make application development faster and more efficient.

Data can be stored on a variety of third-party relational database vendor packages. The interface between PowerBuilder and the DBMS you choose is simple to install and powerful.

Furthermore, PowerBuilder was designed to take advantage of client/server applications technology. In other words, the data stored on the relational DBMS can be local or remote to the application, without requiring the application itself to be aware of the data's location. PowerBuilder and the DBMS interface manage data location, storage, and retrieval, and keep DBMS management totally independent from GUI application development.

PRODUCT FEATURES

Database administration via a single graphical interface regardless of backend DBMS.

Graphical construction of SQL queries through a point-and-click interface.

Easy-to-use, powerful screen painting facility to create and maintain graphical common user interface (CUA) standard interfaces supporting all Microsoft Windows controls and features.

Object-oriented development of custom user objects, featuring inheritance, polymorphism, and encapsulation. Code is stored in libraries that allows it to be shared across applications. Applications are "event-driven," which minimizes the amount of code required to perform fixed tasks.

A powerful, BASIC-like programming language, called PowerScript, to code application logic.

The PowerBuilder DataWindow—a proprietary window object that can be used to perform complex database manipulation easily.

Complete support for standard interface technologies, including dynamic data exchange (DDE), object linking and embedding (OLE), and external function calls in dynamic link libraries (DLL).

Ability to import data from other DBMS formats, such as Lotus, DBase, and others.

Integrated application debugger that allows the programmer to step through PowerBuilder scripts and quickly find problems or insure application integrity.

Extensive and complete on-line help.

A powerful database facility with Powersoft's acquisition of the Watcom SQL product.

WHAT POWERBUILDER DOES FOR YOU

Offers rapid prototype development where prototype code is not lost and can eventually evolve into the finished application.

Provides the ability to implement staged client/server architecture, that is, develop an application as stand-alone (application and database are both local) and move to a distributed database environment by simply changing the configuration, not recoding the application.

Enables the development of easy-to-use, creative, attractive applications under Microsoft Windows which can take advantage of all Windows features and integrate fully with other applications.

Uses event-driven and object-oriented applications. Both of these concepts minimize the amount of necessary applications code and maximize the ability of a shop to maintain applications easily.

Provides a graphical development environment that lowers programmer learning curves and allows the application user community to get involved with application development on new levels.

Contains powerful production reporting tools.

PowerBuilder Terms

PowerBuilder is an easy way to generate powerful Microsoft Windows applications that access your client or server database. This chapter deals specifically with the concepts of window controls and objects. You will learn the procedures and features in Windows applications, and also about other controls that are placed on windows. You will also learn about the various potential components of a window, such as system menus, menu bar, and menu accelerators. Different types of windows will be introduced and reviewed, and you will learn the different ways windows relate to each other.

PowerBuilder applications are event-driven. You will learn how event-driven programming makes it easier to build applications with PowerBuilder. You will learn the concepts of object-oriented programming—inheritance, polymorphism, and encapsulation.

In addition, the concepts of external communications and external functions will be presented.

WHAT ARE WINDOWS APPLICATIONS?

Windows applications are programs written for the Windows environment, using the methods of pull-down menus, icons, and point-and-click procedures. Each window has a title bar and may also have such features as vertical and horizontal scroll bars, a menu bar, maximize and minimize buttons, and a control-menu box. You can change the position or the size of the window using the mouse.

WINDOWS APPLICATION DEVELOPMENT

General Windows Concepts

> ***Graphical User Interface (GUI)*** Using graphics and symbols in a mouse-driven, full-color screen-based environment to create flexible screens or windows to collect or display data in a point-and-click fashion. Take action by clicking on icons (pictures), data, or pushbuttons, or by choosing from pull-down menus.
>
> ***Common User Access (CUA)*** A set of published rules reflecting a common standard across GUI applications, and suggesting methodology for creating a GUI interface and defining how the interface should react to specific user actions. By following the CUA standards, your application will be very similar to other Windows applications in both function and appearance. This lowers the learning curve for your application, as a user will already be familiar with application navigation schemes and will know where to look for help.
>
> ***Control*** Control refers to a graphical object, which can be a window or a singular object that sits on a window, such as an entry field, a check box, a list box, an icon, or a pull-down menu.

Windows and Controls

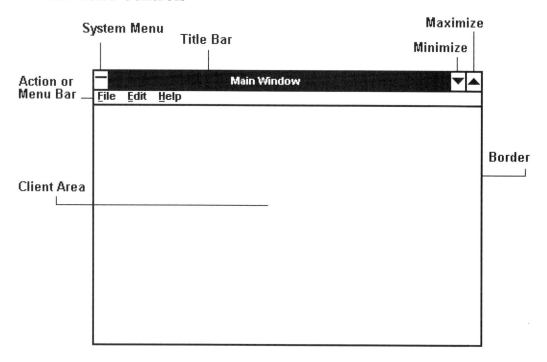

Window The primary control in a GUI application. The window is made up of various potential components. Standard windows have the following features:

System Menu The small box in the upper lefthand corner (looks like a dash) gives access to the system menu functions for the window. Functions such as restore, move, size, maximize, and minimize may be made available to the user here.

Minimize/Maximize Buttons These two buttons in the upper righthand corner of the window are used to size the window. The down arrow reduces the box to an icon; the up arrow makes the box the original size before being minimized.

Title Bar The title bar is the area between the system menu button and the minimize/maximize buttons. It contains the window title and is also used to move the window (drag it to a new location).

Window Border   The window border is changeable—choices are single, double, and sizable window.

Menu Bar (or Action Bar)   The menu bar is commonly located under the title bar, and it contains access to pull-down application menus. The choices displayed are CUA standard (File—with options such as New, Open, Save, Delete, etc.; Edit—with options such as Cut, Paste, Copy, etc.; Help).

Menu Accelerators   Menu choices usually have menu accelerators associated with them, which are identified by the underscore under one letter of the menu title. The menu accelerator allows the user to press the ALT key and the letter underscored instead of using a mouse.

Application Area   The application area is the white space inside the window frame. The application area contains user controls or other windows.

Window Flavors

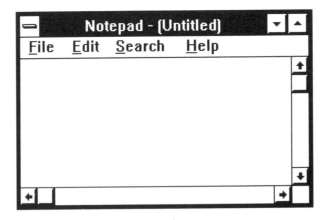

Main Window A standard window—also known as a parent window since it can have child windows—or a main window can stand alone or co-exist on the desktop with other windows. It is independent of all other windows.

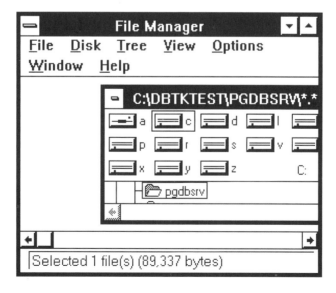

Child Window A window that is dependent on a main or parent window and can only exist and be seen within the boundaries of the main window, a child window automatically moves with its parent and is automatically closed when its parent is closed. When a child window is minimized, it is displayed as an icon within its parent.

Other Window Flavors

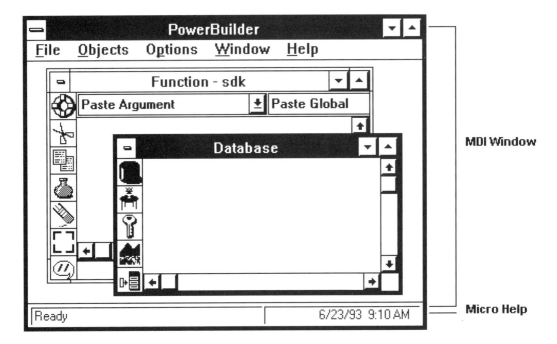

Multiple Document Interface (MDI) Window The MDI window acts as the background or container for all other windows in the application. An MDI window allows multiple windows to be displayed on the desktop under its control, thus allowing the user to switch between MDI child windows. There are two flavors of MDI window: (1) **MDI Window**—A standard MDI window; and (2) **MDIHelp Window**—A standard MDI window with the ability to add a microhelp status line (status line at bottom of MDI window) to give help or status information.

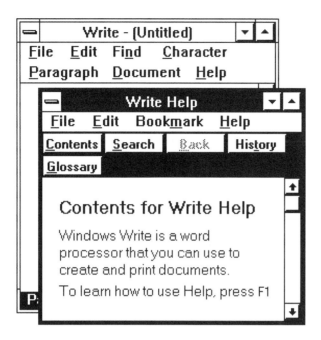

Pop-up Window A type of child window commonly used to display error messages or warnings. It can overlay an existing window and exist outside the boundaries of existing windows.

Response Window Very similar to a pop-up window. It is commonly used to collect important information or get a required response from the user. The response window cannot be closed until the user responds.

Other Window Terms

Window Controls Other controls exist on the application area of a window. These controls are the objects responsible for collecting and displaying data. You have eighteen standard controls at your disposal, and the ability to create your own user controls.

Available Window Controls

Static Text	Horizontal Scroll Bar
Single Line Edit	Vertical Scroll Bar
Check Box	Picture
Radio Button	Oval
Command Button	Rectangle
Picture Button	Line
Group Box	Round Rectangle
MultiLine Edit	
Drop Down List	
List Box	

Special Controls

Data Window
User Controls

Control Attributes Each control has attributes that determine how the control looks, acts, and responds to user action. Attributes for a control include Caption, Size, Location (X and Y coordinates), and Enabled. The programmer will determine the attributes for a control when a window is painted. Control attributes can also be affected programmatically during runtime.

Control Focus When a given window control is the active control, it is said to have "focus." Generally, when a user clicks on a control with the mouse, or TABs to that control, he or she gives that control focus. When a user presses the TAB key, or clicks on another control, the control with focus loses it, and the next control acquires it. Control focus is a critical concept to understand in an event-driven application development environment.

Script A script is the PowerBuilder term for a routine written in PowerScript, the PowerBuilder programming language.

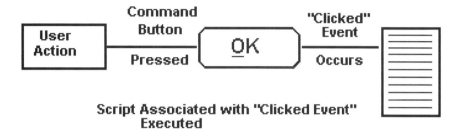

Event-Driven Applications Event-driven programming is the latest concept in simplified application development. Instead of forcing a programmer to code (and recode) everything necessary to produce a window control, the control is already precoded and simply has hooks available to process application-specific code for every event the control can respond to. For example, when a Single Line Edit control is clicked on, the event is "getfocus." When the user presses the TAB key to move to the next control, the event "losefocus" occurs for this control. Other common events include "clicked," "double-clicked," and "modified."

For each event that occurs for a control, the programmer has the option of coding a specific action (using PowerScript) or accepting the default action. This way, all of the code required to display the control and respond (in a default manner) to all pertinent events is already coded for the programmer. The programmer only has to code overrides for the specific events on the specific controls the application *needs* to respond to.

Event-driven application programming also allows the user, instead of the programmer, to control the sequence of processing. The programmer does not need to know, nor does the programmer dictate, the sequence of processing. Processing occurs when the user performs an action or "event" (such as clicking on a control).

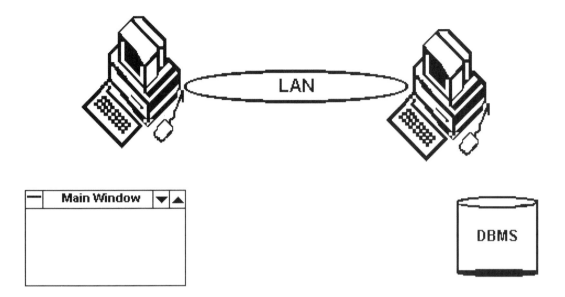

Client/Server This is a term you will hear from time to time; more often as we progress through the nineties. Client/server is a very broad technological concept. For our purposes, it is used to refer to the relationship between the GUI front end (client) and the relational database management system back end (server). The client requests services; the server provides services. The client and server may or may not exist on the same machine or use the same CPU.

Suffice it to say that in a client/server environment, the location of the data should be transparent to the user. The application should not know or care whether the DBMS is on the local hard drive, or actually sitting on a database server somewhere else on the network.

In PowerBuilder, with few exceptions (namely Database Preferences), the programmer will not need to know or care where the DBMS is located. Furthermore, if the DBMS is located on the local drive and is moved to a shared environment on the LAN, there should not be any required *programming* changes.

OBJECT-ORIENTED PROGRAMMING

General Concepts

Object A definable unit of work or process.

Encapsulation The idea that an object is made up of both code and data. The data items and code are encapsulated in the object and do not need to be published to the outside world. All the caller needs to know is the name of the object and the tasks or methods it can perform.

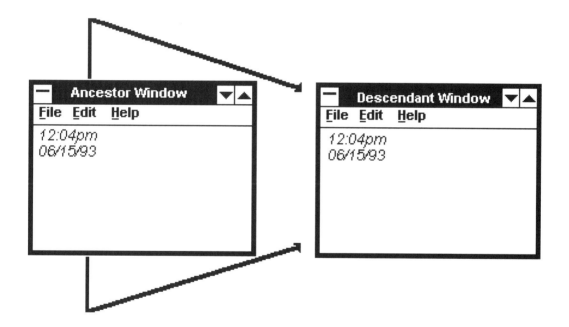

Inheritance The concept of one object being able to inherit another object's characteristics. For example, if a window is developed with certain characteristics (i.e., time and date showing in the upper righthand corner), a second window can be created that inherits the characteristics of the first window. This allows the two windows to share the same code and operate more efficiently.

Polymorphism Once a second window is created with the inherited characteristics of its ancestor, the controls and methods (event scripts) can be overridden to give the second window some of the inherited characteristics while doing some other things differently. This concept is called *polymorphism*.

Instance One manifestation of a class.

Dynamic Binding All objects are defined at runtime and they are linked together to build an application at execution time.

Class Library A library of reusable, tested, code that contains common characteristics with the other program modules in the class.

EXTERNAL COMMUNICATIONS

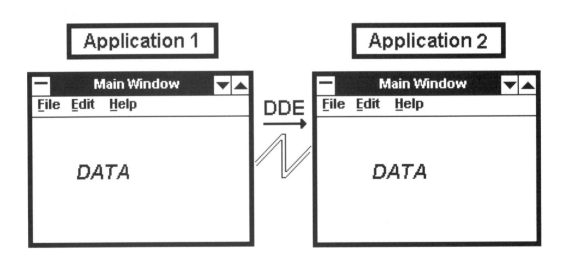

General Concepts

Dynamic Data Exchange (DDE) A way of passing data from one application to another with limited fuss. DDE allows the programmer to establish a link from one application to another and send data from one window to another without user intervention.

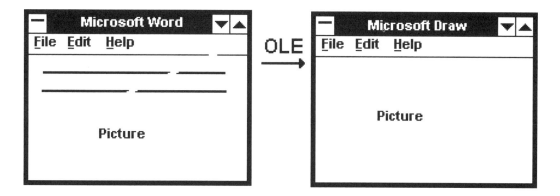

Object Linking and Embedding (OLE) Windows applications can be coded to take advantage of Object Linking and Embedding. OLE allows data that was created in one application to exist in another. Whenever you want to work with that data, OLE dumps you into the application that was used to create the data in the first place. For example, you may want a picture to be included in your Microsoft Word document. Word will dump you into Microsoft Draw to work with the picture and then return you to Word. The picture is stored in your Word document, but Word knows you created the picture in Draw. As a result, if you attempt to modify the picture from your Word document, you will be dumped back into Draw to make the modifications.

External Functions

Dynamic Link Libraries (DLL) Dynamic Link Libraries are a way to share coded routines dynamically between applications. An application program can gain access, at runtime, to an external function that lives in a DLL. The DLL is loaded into memory only once by the operating system and kept in memory as long as one application is using it. Each application requiring the use of any DLL functions can then dynamically link to the DLL and have access to them. A DLL allows functions to be added to an application without having to relink every program which uses the library. A DLL also allows multiple applications to use the functions stored in the library while the library is only loaded once, a much more efficient way to use external functions.

The PowerBuilder Environment

This chapter presents the various icons in the PowerBuilder environment. When opened, the first window in PowerBuilder displays a menu bar and the PowerBar. The icons on the PowerBar and in the PowerPanel symbolize each of the main painters and tools used in PowerBuilder.

In addition, we will discuss saving objects, such as menus and windows, in a PowerBuilder Library (.pbl file). Different painters in PowerBuilder provide a variety of tools for building objects—there is a separate painter for each type of object you want to build.

POWERBUILDER APPLICATIONS

Application Processing

In a PowerBuilder application, processing is event-driven: What this means is that when a user clicks on button 2 and then button 1, the processing associated with button 2 takes place first. The two buttons are independent of each other. Processing can be associated with a number of things—the application, a window, or objects in a window.

POWERBUILDER ENVIRONMENT

PowerBuilder Power Panel

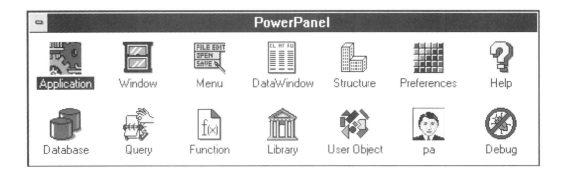

Each icon represents one of the PowerBuilder painters, and the features of each one are described in the following text.

Icons

Application Painter

- Creates a PowerBuilder application library
- Sets up application default fonts and colors
- Codes script for application events via the Script painter
- Builds application executable file
- Sets up default application

Window Painter

- Constructs windows with the controls and objects that make up the window
- Accesses the Script painter for coding PowerBuilder script
- Handles the bulk of development activity

Menu Painter

- Creates menus that can be attached to a window
- Accesses the Script painter to code menu script

DataWindow Painter

A DataWindow is a specialized object that manipulates data from a relational database without coding SQL commands.

- Builds DataWindow objects that can be placed on a window
- Provides multiple presentation styles: tabular, grid, freeform, crosstag, graph, group, label, n-up

Structure Painter

Structures may consist of variables of the same or different data types.

- Defines program structures
- Allows variable(s) to be referenced by a structure name
- Facilitates communication with external programs

Preference Painter

The Preference painter generally requires the following information: DBMS-specific data Vendor, DBMS, LogId, LogPassword, ServerName (if connecting to LAN file server), default database, and Login information: LogId, LogPassword, UserId, and DatabasePassword.

- Establishes customized default information for the Power-Builder environment

Help

Context-sensitive help is available in the development environment. The developer may add help text for help on user objects, events or functions.

Database Painter

- Creates and maintains tables, indexes, and views
- Retrieves and manipulates database data
- Controls database access
- Paints SQL statements and used for immediate execution

Query Painter

- Creates SQL SELECT statements for reuse with DataWindows objects
- Selects tables and columns, and defines sorting and grouping criteria, computed columns, etc.

Function Painter

- Develops user-defined functions
- Uses PowerScript, PowerBuilder's scripting language, to code functions

Library Painter

- Creates and maintains PowerBuilder libraries (.pbl)
- Provides check-in/check-out facility to manage multiple developer environments
- Produces detailed reports on PowerBuilder libraries and their components

User Object Painter

- Creates user-defined objects from standard windows controls, external custom objects, previously defined user objects, or a combination of the above
- Defines user object attributes, events, scripts and functions

Run/Test/Current Application

- Executes the current application from within the PowerBuilder development environment

Debug

- Executes PowerBuilder script in Debug mode
- Examines and modifies variables
- Uses step-through script
- Sets Breakpoints

POWERBUILDER APPLICATION FILES

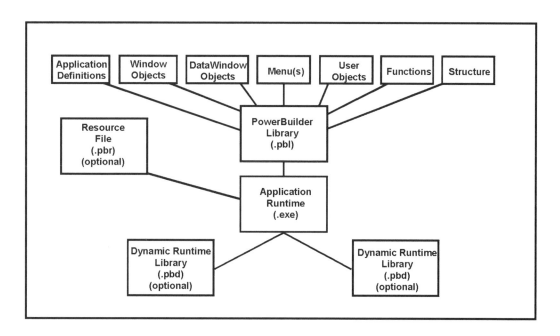

PowerBuilder Application Library (.pbl)

PowerBuilder uses libraries as repositories to store objects with their scripts as compiled definitions. The application library is created in the Application painter, then library maintenance is performed in the Library painter.

Resource File (.pbr) (Optional)

Because resources are assigned dynamically, PowerBuilder cannot identify resources when it builds the .exe. The .pbr file lists the names of these resources and must be referenced when creating the .exe, so you should list names of the resources you want included with the .exe. The resource file also contains the ASCII file in which you list resource names such as .bmp, .cur, .ico, .rle files and DataWindow objects. Any ASCII text editor can be used to create the resource file.

Dynamic Runtime Library (.pbd) (Optional)

The Dynamic Runtime Library is a library that is called dynamically at runtime to load windows, user objects, menus, or DataWindows. It allows you to break the application into smaller, easier-to-manage units that make the .exe smaller.

PowerBuilder Executable (.exe)

The PowerBuilder .exe file is created in the Application painter and contains the following:

A PowerBuilder runtime bootstrap routine
The application icon
The compiled version of each object in the application

COMPONENTS OF A POWERBUILDER APPLICATION

A PowerBuilder application consists of objects, events, and scripts.

Object

An object is a way of communicating with the user (a window or a menu).

Event

An event takes place when the user executes an action. Power-Script statements and the system itself can also cause an event to happen. Some typical events include:

Clicking
Double-Clicking
Modify
Open
Close

Script

Written in the PowerScript language, a script describes the processing that takes place. PowerBuilder executes the script for an event and object or control.

STEPS IN CREATING A POWERBUILDER APPLICATION

1. **Preferences**

   a. Set up vendor-specific DBMS-related parameters.
   b. Set up Login information

2. **Database Painter**

   a. Create database, tables, indexes
   b. Assign table permissions (database access levels)

3. **Application Painter**

   a. Create application library
   b. Add library to the list of libraries that make up your application
   c. Set application defaults—fonts, colors, icon, etc.
   d. Code application level script (e.g., open(w_main_window))

    e. Designate the application as the default application for your PowerBuilder sessions

4. Window Painter

    a. Select *new* to create a new window or select *window* from list to modify
    b. Select controls for the window
    c. Assign properties for each control
    d. Code event-driven script for each control

5. Menu Painter

    a. Paint menu
    b. Code event-driven script for the menu selections
    c. Return to Window painter and attach the menu to the window

6. Testing/Debugging

    a. Select the appropriate testing tool
    b. Debug—step through code, set stops, watch or effect variables, etc.
    c. Execute inside Window painter
    d. Click on the run icon on the Power Panel

7. Library Painter

    a. Optimize PowerBuilder Application Library (.pbl)
    b. Build .pbd's (if applicable)

8. Return to Application Painter

    a. Build application .exe for execution
    b. Application is ready for distribution

The final step is installing the PowerBuilder runtime files and adding the application .exe to the user's desktop.

COMPONENTS OF A WINDOW

A window is the foundation of the application and the key connection with the user.

Controls

Controls are objects placed in a window and defined in the Window painter itself, and not other painters. Some typical controls include:

CheckBox	CommandButton
DataWindow	DropDownListBox
EditMask	GroupBox
HScrollBar	VScroll Bar
MultiLineEdit	User object
Picture	RadioButton
SingleLineEdit	ListBox

Initiate Focus

Focus identifies where on the screen the next action will take place. To initiate focus:

a. Move the mouse cursor to the control button and click, or
b. Press the Tab key until the control button is selected

A control can lose focus when the user:

a. Clicks on another control button, or
b. Presses the Tab key

Attributes

Each object and control has attributes that define its appearance and behavior. The *height* and *width* attributes for a Command-

Button define its appearance, and the *visible* and *enabled* attributes define its behavior.

Using Functions

There are three basic way to use functions:

a. Alone
b. Assigning the return value to a variable
c. In a flow of control structure

To use the return value, the PowerScript statement that calls the function must provide a place for the returned value to be stored, or immediately pass the result to a function, expression, or other language facility.

```
variable = FunctionName(parameter,...)+constant+...
```

To ignore the return value, enter the function call as a statement by itself:

```
FunctionName(parameter,...)
```

Note: User-defined functions may have a return type of NONE.

4

PowerBuilder Preferences

This chapter will explain what preferences are and how they are used. For all of the Preferences that can be set for the various options, the primary values have been included here. Complete information about any and all preference values can be found in the online Help for the preferences for each particular painter.

SETTING PREFERENCES IN POWERBUILDER

Preferences are set for and saved with each application; they are global variables that effect how the various PowerBuilder painters operate. Preferences allow the programmer to set application defaults, and they are particularly important to DBMS operation—they determine what DBMS is used. If the data is remote, preferences are used to tell PowerBuilder where data is located and how to attach to a remote database.

Preferences can be set from each individual painter or by doubleclicking on the Preferences icon on the Power Panel. Preference information is stored in pb.ini file. The location of this file can be specified or changed by adding the following lines to win.ini:

```
[PowerBuilder]
INITPATH=D:\DirectoryName
```

Certain information requires a manual variable be entered in pb.ini in order to store the data portion and use the specific feature. Specific features are specified for the following major categories, with each category being enclosed in brackets ([ ]) in the pb.ini file:

[pb]

[application]

[data window]

[database]

[window]

[menu]

[library]

[script]

[debug]

[DBMS_PROFILES]

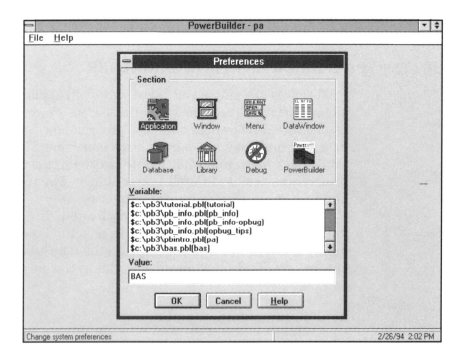

How to Set Preferences

  a. Click on the icon for the painter preferences you wish to view or change

  b. The list of available variables will change by function

  c. Click on the variable whose value you wish to view

  d. The value field will change depending upon which variable is active

Note: Not all preferences and their values have been included in this document. Online Help and the software reference materials will have information on any not included here.

APPLICATION PAINTER PREFERENCES

AppName—Default Application Name This variable contains the name of the application you want to be active (loaded) when a PowerBuilder session is started.

  Example: *testapp*
       Makes *testapp* the default application.

AppLib—Application Library This variable contains the name of the library where the default application resides.

  Example: *d:\pb\testapp.pbl*
       Looks to *testapp.pbl* located in the pb subdirectory of the d drive for the application library.

DefLib—Default Library This variable contains the name of the default library where all objects will be stored. You can override this location when you save an object.

  Example: *d:\pb\testapp.pbl*
       Looks to *testapp.pbl* located in the pb subdirectory of the d drive for the default library.

Library Search Path This variable contains the list of library files that will be searched, in the order they will be searched at runtime for application objects. This variable is stored for each PowerBuilder application.

Example: *d:\pb\testapp.pbl*

WINDOW PAINTER PREFERENCES

GridON This option will turn the placement grid on (value 1) or off (value 0). If the grid is on, when a control is placed on the window, the control is snapped to the grid. The default is 0.

GridShow This option will display the placement grid (value 1) or hide the grid (value 0). The default is 1.

GridX This variable determines the width of the placement grid in pixels. The default is 8.

GridY This variable determines the height of the placement grid in pixels. The default is 8.

Status This variable controls whether the status of the currently selected object should be displayed in the status window. The default (value 0) is DO NOT DISPLAY the status window; to display the window change the value to 1.

Default3D This variable determines if controls are displayed in 3D or normal. Default is NO (normal).

MENU PAINTER PREFERENCES

Prefix A menu is nothing more than another control. This variable contains the prefix given to menu controls.

DATAWINDOW PAINTER PREFERENCES

GridON This option will turn the placement grid on (value 1) or off (value 0). If the grid is on, when a control is placed on the window, the control is snapped to the grid. The default is 0.

GridShow This option will display the placement grid (value 1) or hide the grid (value 0). The default is 1.

GridX This variable determines the width of the placement grid in pixels. The default is 8.

GridY This variable determines the height of the placement grid in pixels. The default is 8.

Ruler This variable determines if rulers will display in the workspace. NO hides the rulers. The default is NO.

Status This variable controls whether the status of the currently selected object should be displayed in the status window. The default (Value 0) is DO NOT DISPLAY the Selected Object Status Window; to display the window, change this variable to 1.

Outline Objects This variable determines if the outline of objects in the DataWindow will be displayed. Selecting 1 displays outlines; 0 does not display.

PreviewRetrieve This variable controls whether data is immediately retrieved when a Preview DataWindow Report or Object is selected. Selecting 0 executes retrieve only after Retrieve button is clicked; selecting 1 executes retrieve immediately. The default is 1.

PreviewOnNew This variable determines whether to go immediately to the Print Preview window after creating a new Data Window Definition.

PrintPreviewRulers This variable controls whether rulers will be displayed on print preview. The default is NO.

PrintPreviewZoom This variable controls the zoom percentage for Print Preview. The default is 100 percent.

Other Preferences

```
new_default_presentation
new_default_datasource
new_nup_text_color
new_nup_column_color
new_nup_color
new_nup_text-border
new_nup_column_header
```

For complete information about these preferences, access the online Help system for DataWindows preferences.

DATABASE PAINTER PREFERENCES

Vendors This preference displays the name of the DBMS PowerBuilder should have access to. There may be multiple vendors listed here; the default DBMS should be listed first, the rest should be listed and separated by commas.

DBMS This preference displays the name of the default DBMS vendor (i.e., the first vendor listed in the Vendors variable).

LogId This preference displays the Logon ID PowerBuilder has to use to get past DBMS security (during connects)—*required for SQLServer, MDI, and Oracle Server.*

LogPassword This preference displays the Logon Password PowerBuilder has to use to get past DBMS security (during connects)—*required for SQLServer, MDI, and Oracle Server.*

ServerName This preference displays the Network Name of the server your database is located on. This is the 8-character server name (not the network path to the server)—*required for SQLServer, MDI, and Oracle Server.*

Database This preference displays the name of the database used by this application.

UserId This preference displays the name of the User ID required for **database** security.

Database Password This preference displays the password required for **database** security.

Lock This preference defines the isolation level.

Columns This preference shows the maximum number of columns displayed when you expand a table or view. If the number of columns exceeds this number, a horizontal scroll bar appears.

StayConnected This variable allows you to specify whether PowerBuilder connects to the DBMS when a painter requests it and stays connected until you exit PowerBuilder (Value 1), or simply connects when you enter a painter and disconnects when you leave the painter (Value 0). The default is 1.

DBParm This variable is database-dependent and displays only after *you* create a DBParm variable in pb.ini. It allows for parameters to be passed to the database at connect time.

TableDir This variable determines if the database painter will automatically display a list of tables in the current database (Value 1). The other option (Value 0) means you have to click on the database icon in the toolbar to get a list of tables. The default is 1.

Other Preferences

```
AutoCommit
TerminatorCharacter
ShowRefInt
ShowIndexKeys
IndexKeyLineColor
PrimaryKeyLineColor
ForeignKeyLineColor
Prompt
```

For complete information about these preferences, access the online Help system for Database Painter Preferences.

LIBRARY PAINTER PREFERENCES

The library painter allows you to print developer reports against your application libraries. These reports can be very useful in tracking product development and for documentation. The library preference variables determine what information is displayed and how it is displayed. See PowerBuilder online Help or documentation for detailed information.

DeletePrompt This variable controls whether to prompt for delete or not. Selecting 1 turns prompt on; selecting 0 turns prompt off.

SourceVendor This variable displays the ID of the Source Control Vendor (e.g., PVCS).

CondensedFont This variable controls whether a condensed font will be used for reports.

NormalFont This variable contains the normal font for your printer.

DEBUG PAINTER PREFERENCES

Stopn This variable identifies the stops set in Debug.

VariablesWindow This variable controls the display of the Variables Window. Selecting 1, yes, displays the variables window; 0, no, does not. The default is 0.

WatchWindow This variable controls the display of the Watch Window. Selecting 1, yes, displays the watch window; 0, no, does not. The default is 0.

POWERBUILDER PREFERENCES

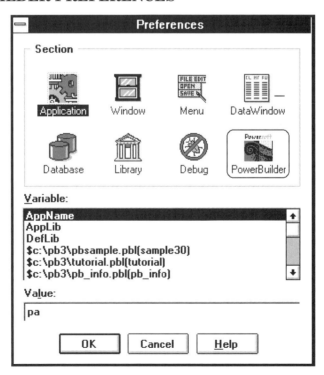

Power Panel This variable determines whether the Power Panel Mode (1) or Power Bar Mode (2) will be used. The default is 1.

Maximized This variable determines whether PowerBuilder windows will be maximized on display (Value 1), or whether to display each window in the same size and position they were last created (Value 0).

Layer This variable determines whether PowerBuilder Windows will be layered (Value 1) or cascaded (Value 0).

Window This variable contains the display size and position for the last creation of PowerBuilder windows.

Other Preferences

```
SharedIni                FontName
PromptOnExit             Object1
ToolBarFontName          Object2
ToolBarFontHeight        Object3
FontHeight               Object4
FontBold                 Toolbar Text
FontFace
FontName
```

For complete information about these preferences, access the online Help system for PowerBuilder preferences.

5

PowerBuilder Application Painter

After completing this chapter, you will be able to add or change PowerBuilder application libraries. You will learn how to build a new application, how to set up an application library search path. We will explain how to change text default fonts, style, size, and colors. You will learn what tasks can be accomplished through the Application painter. In addition, the Painter Bar controls, their defaults, and how to use them will be discussed.

ACCESSING THE APPLICATION PAINTER

Power Panel

Choose the application painter icon from the Power Panel or PowerBar.

PowerBar

PowerPanel

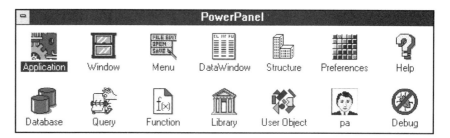

Workspace

To see the Application painter workspace, double-click on the application painter icon either in the PowerBar or Power Panel.

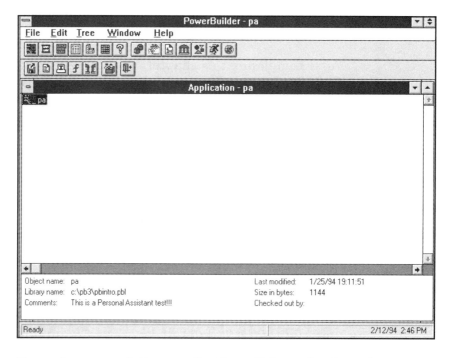

To work on an existing application, click on the Open button.

APPLICATION PAINTER

By double-clicking on the application painter icon on the Power Panel, then selecting File/Open from the Menu, or the Open button on the painter bar, you will receive the Select Application window. The Select Application window displays:

Name of the current directory (drive and path)

List of libraries (.pbl's) in that directory

Drives and subdirectories currently available

Current application library, if one has been previously selected

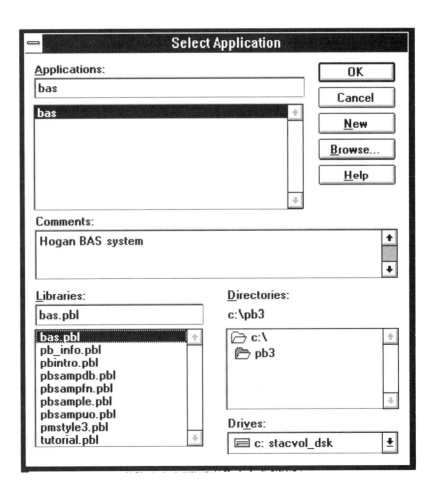

The current library, directory, and drives are defaults. To change the active drive and directory path defaults, select from the applicable list. The Browse pushbutton is used for browsing all active libraries (.pbl's) for an application variable, window name, and the like.

HOW TO CREATE A NEW APPLICATION

1. To build a new application, press the New button on the select application window. This will present the Save Application window.

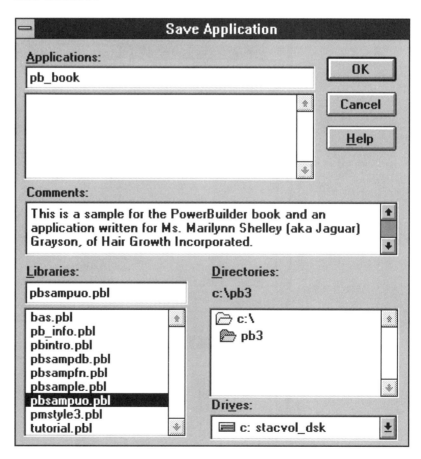

2. Enter the name of your application in the Applications box—the name can be 1 to 40 characters long.
3. Enter the name of your library (if different than the application name). PowerBuilder will generate a name from the first eight characters of the application and add the .pbl extension.
4. Enter any comments to document the application library you are creating.
5. Select the OK pushbutton. The application library will be created.
6. From this point on, you will be working from the painter bar to modify the attributes of the application.

THE PAINTERBAR

The PainterBar may be displayed when you enter the application painter. It can appear at the top, bottom, either side of the screen, or float on the screen. If you cannot see the PainterBar, you can bring it up by selecting Windows/Toolbars from the menu.

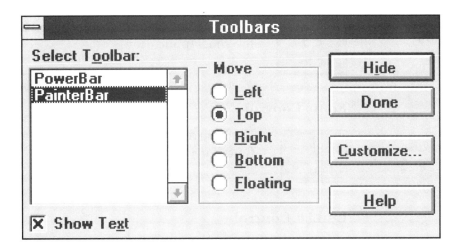

Select PainterBar from the above window. You may display text with the controls or pictures only, as you prefer. Decide where you want to see the PainterBar and click on Done.

PainterBar Controls

Open Control

   Clicking on this control will allow you to select the application you wish to modify.

Script Control

   Clicking on this control allows you to develop a script for your application.

Icon Control

   Clicking on this control allows you to select an icon for your application.

Fonts Control

   Clicking on this control allows you to select default fonts for your application.

LibList Control

   Clicking on this control allows you to select the libraries to be used by your application.

CreateExe Control

Clicking on this control will take you to the window to create the executable for your application.

Return Control

Clicking on this control takes you back to the Application painter.

MODIFYING THE APPLICATION

Selecting an Application Icon

Click the Icon control from the PainterBar. You will see the Select Icon window.

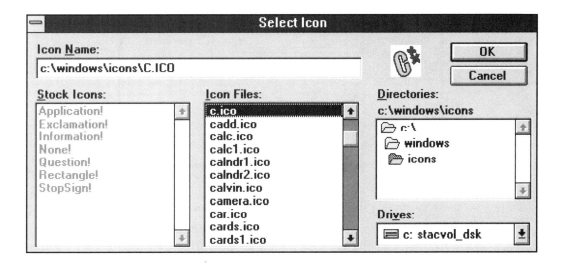

PowerBuilder has a few icons to choose from, or you can use the icons in another directory by selecting the appropriate directory. If you do not select an icon, the run icon will be used as a default. The OK pushbutton will return.

Setting the Application's Default Fonts

Click the Font control from the painter bar to get the Select Default Fonts window.

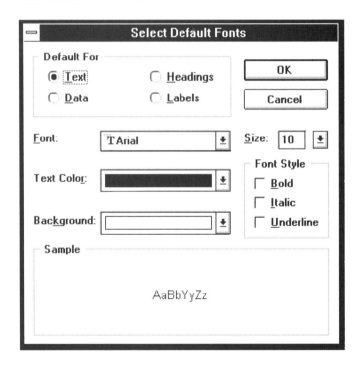

The default fonts, style, size, and colors can be set from this window. These defaults will be applied throughout the application. The defaults set here can be overridden during application development or changed at runtime. The OK pushbutton will return.

Setting up the Application Library Search Path

Click the LibList control from the painter bar to get the Select Libraries window.

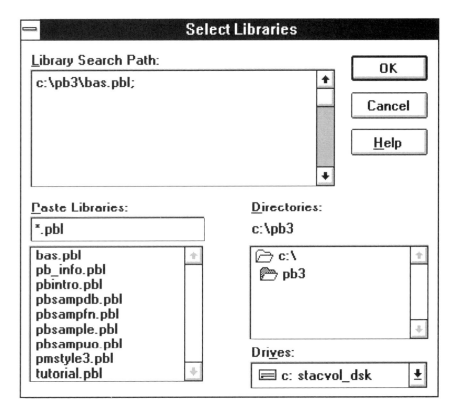

The Library Search Path is a list of libraries that will be searched to find the application objects necessary. The Paste Libraries section contains a list of libraries that can be added to the Library Search Path. The OK pushbutton will return.

Coding Application Level Scripts

Application level scripts are scripts that react to Application Events and Application Related Functions. For example, when a user clicks on an application icon the open event occurs. The script for the open event must be coded, and it usually opens the first window.

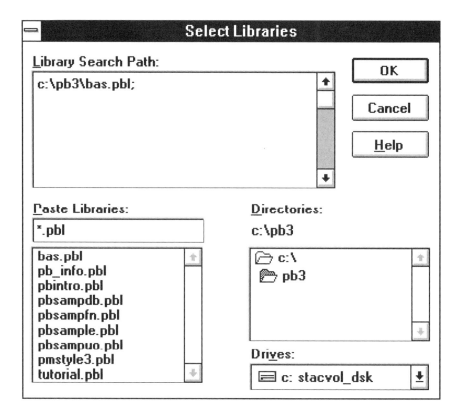

Select the Script control from the painter bar to code scripts that will apply to the Application object. Details follow in chapter 9.

APPLICATION EVENTS AND RELATED FUNCTIONS

Events

The following table lists the events that can occur in an Application object. The script for the open event is the only script required.

Event	Occurs When
Close	The user closes the application. A script can be coded to handle shutdown operations.
Idle	The idle function has been called and the specified number of seconds have elapsed with no mouse or keyboard activity. A script could be coded to handle idle activities.
Open	The user runs the application. Usually, an initialization script is coded here.
SystemError	Serious runtime error has occurred. The script for this event the script is executed if there is one, otherwise a messagebox with the error number and text are displayed. An error handling routine can be coded here.

Related Functions

Application-related functions are functions that cause an application-level event. The table below lists the application-related functions.

Function	Purpose
Idle	Starts a timer that triggers an idle event after a period of user inactivity. The timer is reset after every user activity (mouse move or keystroke).
SignalError	Causes a SystemError at the application level.
TriggerEvent	Starts an event in an application object and executes the associated script.

PowerBuilder Database Painter

The capabilities of the PowerBuilder Database Painter are numerous, and most of your database work will be done in the PowerBuilder Database Painter. In this chapter you will learn how to create, modify, and drop tables; you will create a validation rule and understand how it is used. In addition, you will understand the content and structure of the PowerBuilder system tables, which can be opened and worked with just as any other table. PowerBuilder generates a DataWindow to match the definition of the table to add data to, modify, or delete data from. You will learn how to access the preview feature to obtain data manipulation for your tables.

This chapter will also define extended attributes and where they are stored.

PowerPanel						
Application	Window	Menu	DataWindow	Structure	Preferences	Help
Database	Query	Function	Library	User Object	bas	Debug

You must administer your database from a common interface *regardless* of which DBMS package you are using. You can perform the following tasks with the database painter:

Create, modify, and drop table, index, and view objects

Add and drop primary keys

Control access rights for users against a database

Add extended table definition information for use in Power-Builder programming

Add or modify data

INITIAL TABLE SELECTION

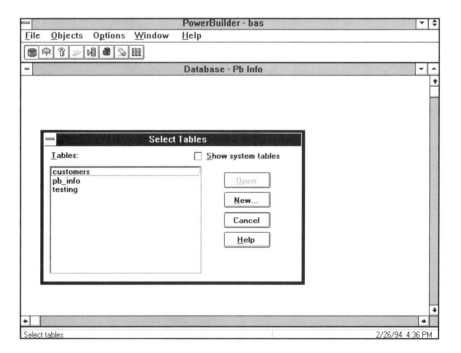

Choose table(s) or view(s) from the table list you wish to work with. You can choose several. Click on Open to open the table(s)/View(s) and move their definitions to the database painter desktop, or click on New to create a new table directly.

Tips

> Changing databases, database type, database Login: Use the
> File pulldown menu from the database painter menu bar
>
> For a list of available functions: Try the Options pulldown menu

DATABASE PAINTER PAINTERBAR

> Once in the database painter, you will use the PainterBar to
> initiate most of the functions. Other functions will be accessed
> from the pulldown menus.

CREATING A NEW TABLE IN POWERBUILDER

> When Select Tables list is displayed, click on New, click on Cre-
> ate New Table Icon on toolbar, or click on Objects pulldown menu
> and choose Create New Table. Then follow these steps:

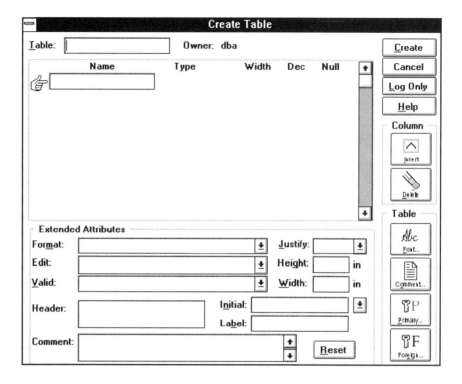

1. Give the table a name.
2. Define each column (name, type, width, decimal, nulls allowed, extended attributes).
3. Add table comment (Comment . . .).
4. Change fonts for display of data, heading, and labels (Font . . .).
5. Define the primary and foreign keys for the table (Primary . . . , Foreign . . .).
6. Use Create to create table now, Log Only to simply save all necessary data definition language (DDL) for later use.

Defining Extended Attributes for a Column

An extended attribute is data managed and stored by PowerBuilder for use in printing and manipulating table data. Extended attributes can be added to the table description at the time the table is created or after opening an existing table.

Format Determines how a column is displayed in the DataWindow. Standard values are: Format Mask, Justify, Display Height, Width, and Case. For complete information on display rule, see Appendix C of the PowerBuilder function reference. Use the Display button to create new display rules.

Edit Controls how the data will appear to the user.

Validation Rule A rule you create that will be used to validate the data entered for this column in a DataWindow. Note: This is a PowerBuilder validation rule, not a database validation rule. Use the Validate button to create new validation rules.

Header The text displayed in a tabular or grid DataWindow for this column. Determine if text is centered, left- or right-justified.

Comment Add extended attribute comments.

Justify Controls data justification. Values are right, left, and centered.

Height/Width Determine the height and width of the column display.

Initial Value The prefilled value in this column in a DataWindow. Standard values are: Spaces, NULL or zeros, or a specific value you choose.

Label The text displayed in a freeform DataWindow for this column. Determine if the text is left- or right-justified.

Input Validation Expressions

Validation Rule An expression that can be true or false, used to validate text in a column by defining acceptable entries. A validation rule is stored in the database with a name, then it can be associated with any number of columns. Typical validation rules contain:

- Literals (constants)
- References to the value entered in the column (@name)
- Operators: arithmetic, relational, and logical
- References to functions

Example
```
@salary > 0.00 and @salary < 1000000
len(@ssn) = 9 and isNumber (@ssn)
@col = ^JJH.*
@col = [^JJH}
@col = ^[0-9][0-9]$
```

Creating a Validation Rule

1. Create a validation rule by clicking on the Option menu item as seen in this screen print.

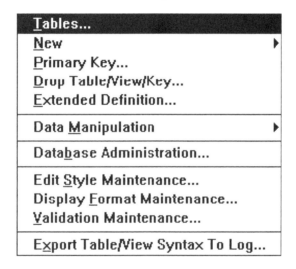

2. Next, select Validation Maintenance and this screen print is
   presented.

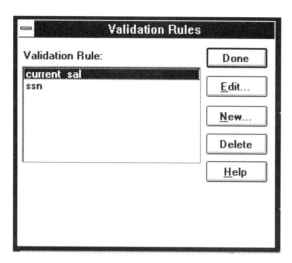

3. Click the NEW button and this screen will be presented.

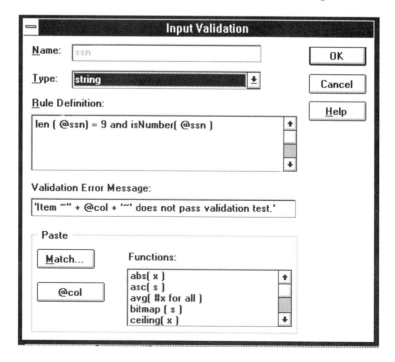

4. Type a name for the validation rule and define the rule and validation error message.

Example Format Expressions

Numeric

0

>   Standard integer format

##0.00

>   Suppress leading zeros and allow for two decimal places

$##,###.00[RED]($##,###.00)

>   Leading dollar sign, suppress leading zeros, two decimal places, and have negative numbers show up in parentheses and in red.

Date/Time

mm/dd/yy

>   Month, two digits, Day, two digits, Year, two digits

dd-mmm-yy

>   Day, two digits, Month, Abbreviation, Year, two digits

mmm dd yyyy hh:mm:ss:ff AM/PM

>   Month fully spelled out; Day, two digits; Year, four digits; Hour, two digits; Minutes, two digits; Seconds, two digits; Fractional seconds, two digits; AM or PM

String

(@@@) @@@-@@@@

>   Phone number format. Area code, prefix, suffix

@@@-@@-@@@@

>   Social Security Number format

See PowerBuilder Manuals for more details.

Create a Display Format

From the Objects menu, access the Display Format Definition window by clicking on Display Format Maintenance.

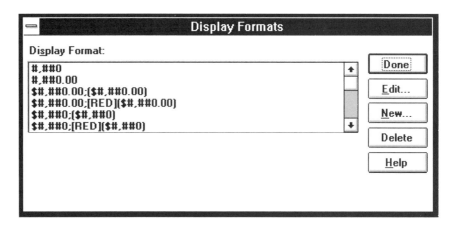

Click on New.

Create an Edit Style

From the popup menu, with the right mouse button select Edit Style, or, select Edit Style Maintenance from the Objects menu. To use an Edit Style already existing, click the style in the Style Names box, then click Done. To create a new Edit Style, click on the New box that shows the correct style.

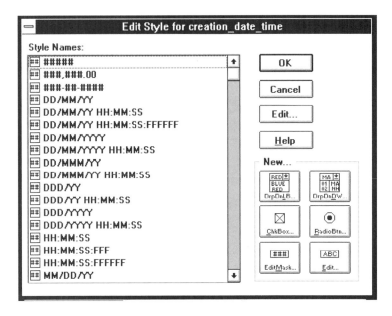

Click on one of the styles.

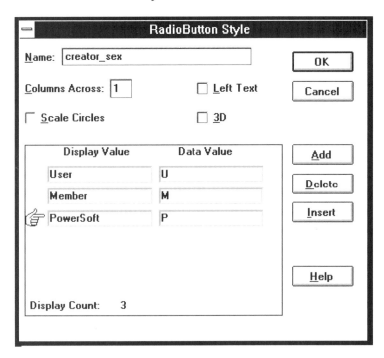

ALTERING TABLES

Altering an existing table can be done by either selecting the Open button from the PainterBar or by selecting the table you wish to modify from the Select Tables window when you first enter the database painter. Highlight the name of the table you want to modify and click on Open. You can also click on New to create a new table.

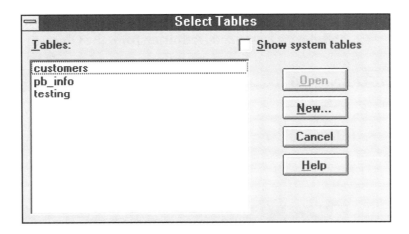

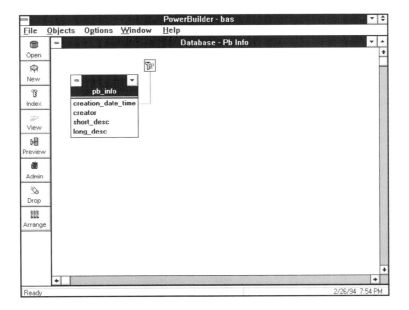

To Show the Current Definition of a Table Click on the maximize button of the table definition you wish to view.

To Alter a Table Definition Double-click on the title bar of the table you wish to alter, or click on the title bar of the table you wish to alter and choose Extended Definition from the Objects pulldown menu.

To Alter a Column's Extended Attributes Double-click on the column you wish to alter, or click on the column you wish to alter and choose Extended Definition from the Objects pulldown menu.

CREATING AN INDEX

Select the table you wish to work with (click on its title bar), and click on the index icon off the tool bar, or choose New/Index off the Objects pulldown menu. Then do the following:

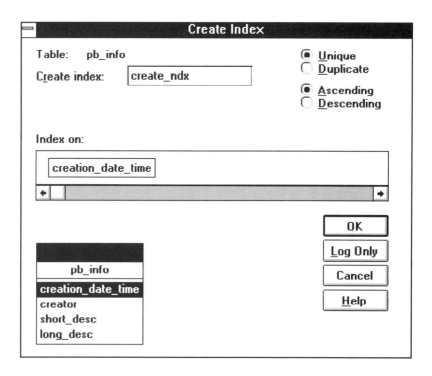

1. Type in index name, choose Unique or Duplicate and Ascending or Descending. NOTE: the choices on this screen are DBMS specific; some DBMSs may offer clustered or unclustered, or other choices.
2. Choose columns in the order you wish to create the index. Column names will be displayed in order of selection in the center entry field.
3. Click on OK to create or Log Only to just create DDL.

The index will show up accordingly.

DELETING TABLES/INDEXES/VIEWS

Choose the table, view, or index you want to delete by making it active (clicking on its representation on the desktop). Then click on the delete icon on the toolbar, or click on Drop Table/View/Index off the Objects pulldown menu.

POWERBUILDER SYSTEM TABLES

To Gain Access to System Tables Click on the Open Painter button to get the Select Tables window, or choose Tables from the Objects pulldown menu. Click on the Show Systems Tables check box on the Select Tables window that follows. Regardless of which DBMS you are using, PowerBuilder always creates four system tables that it maintains:

pbsystablesdict—Information stored about each table, including all general extended attribute information about that table

pbsyscolumnsdict—Information stored about each column in each table, including all column-specific extended attribute information about that column

pbsysformats—All information concerning a particular format rule

pbsysvalids—All information concerning a particular display rule

PowerBuilder system tables can be opened and worked with just as any other table.

ADDING/DELETING/MODIFYING TABLE ROWS

The Preview feature of the PowerBuilder database painter allows you to manipulate data for your tables. PowerBuilder will generate a DataWindow that matches the definition of the table or view you wish to add data to, modify, or delete data from, or simply view the data in.

To Create a DataWindow Against a Table Select the table or view you wish to work with by making it active on the desktop.

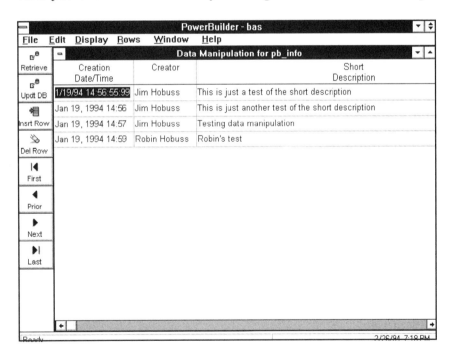

Click on the Preview icon, or choose Data Manipulation from the Objects pulldown menu.

DATA MANIPULATION COMMAND BUTTONS

The PainterBar contains the command buttons for Data Manipulation which allow you to modify your data base in many ways.

PainterBar Command Buttons

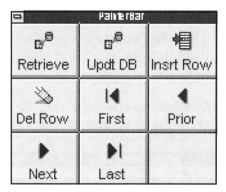

Retrieve

Get all records or records meeting Sort/Validate criteria.

Update DB

Make the update take (commit in effect).

Insert Row

Insert a new row in the database.

Delete Row

Delete current row from the database.

First

Get the first record in the database.

Prior

Get previous record.

Next

Get next record.

Last

Go to the last record on the database.
You can save the DataWindow as an object for use in an application. This can be accomplished from the File pulldown menu. Once a row of data has been entered on the screen, you can save the data from the File pulldown menu. Sorting and filtering criteria as well as importing data into the table can be accomplished from the Row pulldown menu.

7

PowerBuilder Window Painter

This chapter presents the concepts of the PowerBuilder Window painter. The painter has a menu bar, a StyleBar, a customizable PainterBar, a workspace, and a ColorBar. You will learn how to enter the PowerBuilder Window painter and how to create different window types. You will also learn about all of the major controls associated with a PowerBuilder Window. When building a window, you place controls in the window to request and receive information from the user and to present information to the user. This chapter also deals with selecting, sizing, and modifying these controls and the attributes associated with them.

One of the most powerful features of PowerBuilder is inheritance, which permits you to create windows, menus, and user objects from other objects.

USING THE POWERBUILDER WINDOW PAINTER

The Window painter can be used to paint application screens or windows, create different window types, and place controls on windows. It also enables the user to work with window and control attributes, access window and control event scripts and the PowerBuilder debugger.

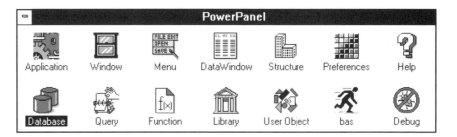

To use the Window Painter, double-click on the Window painter icon.

SELECTING A WINDOW

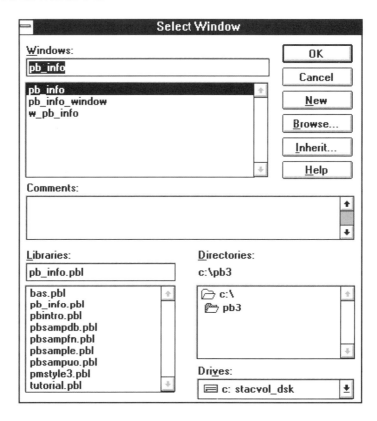

From the top list, choose the name of the existing window you wish to work with, or click on New to create a new window.

Controls

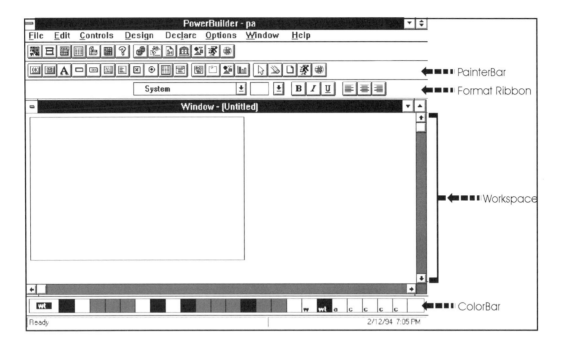

PainterBar The position of the PainterBar on the screen is very versatile: It can be displayed on the top or bottom, on the left or right side, or even in a small window floating freely within the Window painter. Some icons in the PainterBar depict objects or controls that can be added to the window, others represent short-cuts in selecting menu options, or taking action with window objects or controls, or the window itself.

Color Palette Displayed at the bottom of the screen, the Color Palette can change the color of text or drawing objects. There are two ways to change fill or text colors of a control:

1. Select the control, click the right mouse button.
2. Select Color from the popup menu, Background or Text from the cascading menu, and color of choice.

OR

1. Select the control, click the right mouse button in the color palette on the color of choice.
2. Click the secondary mouse button in the color palette on the color of choice to change the color of the border or background.

Format Ribbon   The Format Ribbon is displayed across the top of the window, and is used to change text, font, size, spacing, and right/left justification.

Other Options
Browse   Click on the Browse button to search existing windows for a text string.

Inherit   Click on the Inherit button to choose an existing window to inherit from. Remember, inherit means to start with a window with the same controls (and scripts) as an existing window. Existing controls and attributes can be overridden, but a control inherited from an ancestor cannot be deleted (although you can hide controls you don't wish to use). The default window title will show that this window is in fact inherited from an ancestor. Note: When working with a new or inherited window, we suggest you choose Save As from the File menu and save the new window with a specific name.

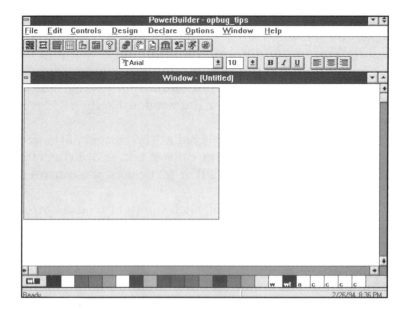

Working with a New Window

To set the font used in a control, choose the font you wish from the Font list box on the Window Painter ribbon; to choose a font pitch used in a control, choose the pitch you wish from the Pitch list box on the Window Painter ribbon. To make the control text you are working with bold, italic, or underlined, press the appropriate pushbutton on the Window painter ribbon, and to left or right adjust or center text, press the appropriate button from the Window painter ribbon.

Setting Window Attributes

To set the attributes of a window, double-click on any piece of white space inside the window control. This will bring up the Window Style window.

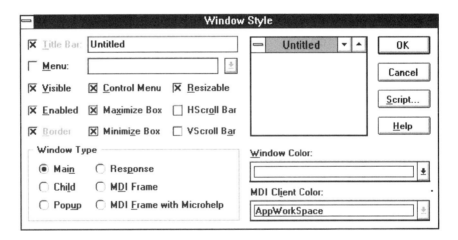

Title Bar If this option is checked, the window will have a title bar. The entry field next to this check box contains the text that will be displayed in the window title bar.

Menu If this option is checked, the window will have a menu. The dropdown list box next to this check box contains the different menu objects available. Choose one.

Visible If this option is checked, the window's default condition is visible.

Enabled If this option is checked, the window's default condition is enabled.

Border If this option is checked, the window will have a border.

 Control Menu If this option is checked, the window will have a control menu available (upper lefthand corner square as default).

 Maximize Box If this option is checked, the window will have a maximize button (upper righthand corner).

 Minimize Box If this option is checked, the window will have a minimize button (upper lefthand corner).

Resizable If this option is checked, the window will be resizable (notice the border style changes with this attribute).

H Scroll Bar If this option is checked, the window will have a horizontal scroll bar.

V Scroll Bar If this option is checked, the window will have a vertical scroll bar.

Window Type Choose window type. This will enable or disable some of the above options. For a review of the different window types available, see previous section on Terms.

Window Color Choose the window background color. Choices include standard window background color (set in native Windows), standard application window background color (set in native Windows), or one of four custom colors.

MDI Client Color If a MDI Frame, select the color scheme to be used. Note: The window displayed in the right corner of the Window Style window will change its appearance depending upon the options chosen.

Other Options Choose the Script button to define a script for the different events relative to the window.

WINDOW TYPES

Main Window

This top-level window is sometimes called a parent window or overlapped window. It is independent of all windows, has a title bar, and can be minimized or maximized.

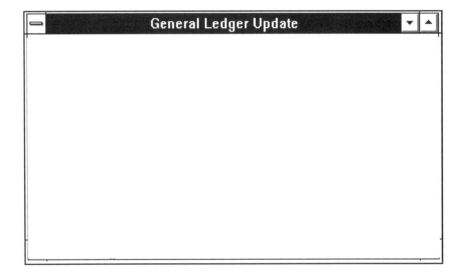

Child Window

Dependent on its parent window, a child window can exist only within the parent window, and is therefore never the active window. It closes and moves with its parent window. A child window can be minimized, but becomes an icon displayed inside the parent window.

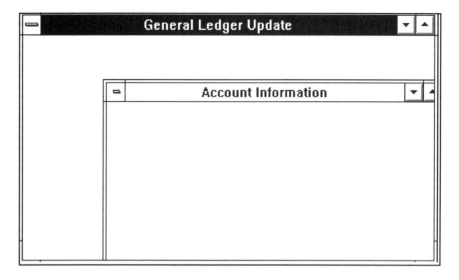

Pop-up Window

A pop-up window can be displayed outside the parent window, but is never hidden behind it. Like a child window, a pop-up window can be minimized and becomes an icon displayed inside the parent window. It may or may not have a title bar.

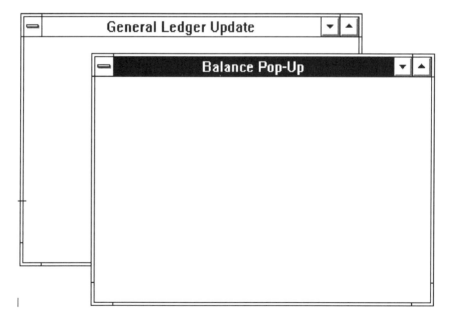

Response Window

When activated, this window obtains or provides information. It remains active until the user responds. While the window is open (application modal):

- The user can go to another window application
- The user cannot go to other windows in the application from which the response window was opened
- The window cannot be minimized

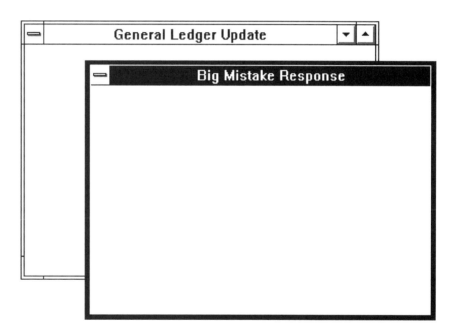

Multiple Document Interface (MDI) Frame

This option permits multiple document windows to display in a cascade, tiled, or layered. The user is allowed to make any document active. It can contain multiple examples of the same or different types of windows.

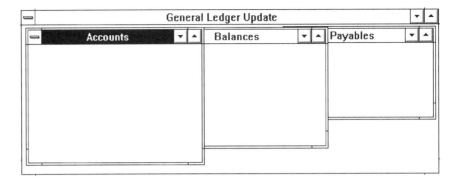

MDI Frame with MicroHelp All characteristics of this option are the same as MDI frame. In addition, it allows the display of MicroHelp information in the status bar.

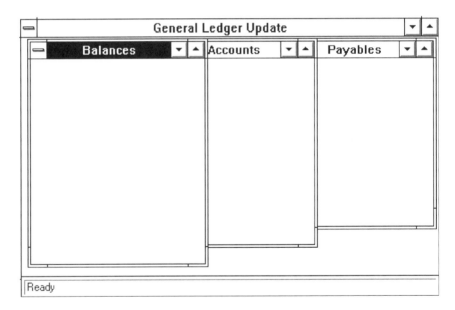

Select Pointer Window

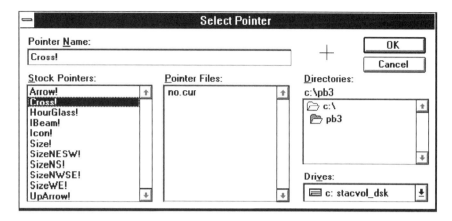

Select Icon Window

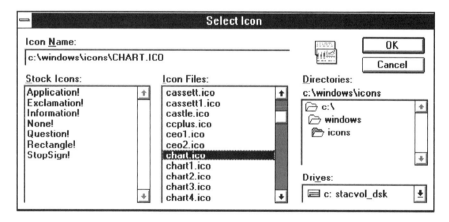

POSITIONING AND SIZING A WINDOW

Window Position

Access the Window Position window by clicking the right mouse button on the window and select Position from the popup menu, or select Window Position from the Design menu.

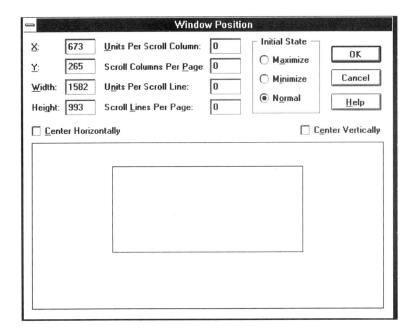

On this screen, you can enter the X and Y coordinates and the Width and Height for the window, or you can place and size the window with the mouse. You can also center the window using the check boxes Center Horizontally and Center Vertically.

CONTROLS

Using Controls

Most of the window controls for creating windows are included on the DataWindow PainterBar. Some of them are only accessible from the Controls Menu item. Some of the controls on the Painter-Bar are not for window controls, but to assist you in defining or testing your window.

Selecting the Control Choose the control you wish to work with from the Window painter toolbar by left clicking over the appropriate icon. Move the mouse pointer to the location on the window where you want the control to be placed. Click the left mouse button to place the control.

Sizing the Control Click on the control to make it active, then move the mouse to one of the control's borders until the mouse becomes a double arrow. Click on the corner of the control with the left mouse button and drag control to the required size.

Moving the Control Click on the control and drag it to its new position.

Changing the Control's Attributes Double-click on the control to bring up a panel to set the default values for the control's attributes.

Setting Values for Controls Position the cursor on the control. Click on the right mouse button to bring up the list of variables to be set or changed.

Common Attribute Options

There are attribute options for most controls that can be set from each control's attribute selection window (accessed by double-clicking on the control).

If there are potential events associated with the control, choose the Script button to define the scripts for the different events.

```
┌─────────────────────────────────────────────────────────┐
│ ⊟               StaticText                                │
├───────────────────────────────────────────┬─────────────┤
│  N̲ame:  │st_display_name              │    │     OK      │
│                                            │             │
│  T̲ext:  │none                         │    │   Cancel    │
│                                            │             │
│  ☒ V̲isible    ☐ E̲nabled    ☐ F̲ocus Rectangle │  S̲cript   │
│                                            │             │
│  B̲order: │None        ±│  A̲lignment: │Center ±│  H̲elp   │
└───────────────────────────────────────────┴─────────────┘
```

Other attributes and functions are available for the controls by positioning the mouse pointer on the control and clicking the right mouse button. Nearly all of the controls have the option of adding a script; all of them have the option to delete or duplicate the control. The following list includes some of the other options; not all options are available for all controls.

Border: Provides the ability to change the border of the control

Change Data Window: Provides the ability to make changes to the data window

Change Disabled: Provides the ability to change the value of the Disabled attribute

Change Enabled: Provides the ability to change the value of the Enabled attribute

Color: Provides the ability to change the color of the control

Drag and Drop: Provides the ability to set the icon associated for drag and drop

Fill Pattern: Provides the value for a fill pattern

Icon: Provides the ability to change the icon associated with the control

Name: Provides the ability to change the name of the control

Pointer: Provides the ability to change to a different icon for the mouse pointer

Style: Provides the ability to change the style

Control Prefixes

Each control that can appear on the window must have a unique name within the window. The system will assign default names using the following standard prefixes:

Standard Control Prefixes

Window Control	w_
Static Text Control	st_
Check Box Control	cbx_
Push Button Control	cb_
Radio Button Control	rb_
Group Box Control	gb_
Single Line Edit Control	sle_
Multi Line Edit Control	mle_
Drop Down List Box Control	ddlb_
List Box Control	lb_
DataWindow Control	dw_
Picture Control	p_
Picture Button Control	pb_
Horizontal Scroll Bar Control	hsb_
Vertical Scroll Bar Control	vsb_
Rectangle Control	r_
Oval Control	oval_
Round Rectangle Control	rr_

Note: While the prefixes can be overridden or the default prefixes changed in painter preferences, it is not recommended.

Static Text Control

This control is used to display static text to the user. Usually used in titles, captions, and instructions.

StaticText		
Name: st_enter_address		OK
Text: none		Cancel
☒ **Visible** ☐ **Enabled** ☐ **Focus Rectangle**		Script
Border: None ▼ **Alignment:** Center ▼		Help

Important Attributes

Name: Unique name (for this window) identifying this control

Text: Assigns the text to be displayed

Visible: Is this control visible (as a default)?

Enabled: Can the value be changed?

Focus Rectangle: Will the dotted rectangle be displayed when this control has focus?

Border: Chooses the border for the control

Alignment: How the text is aligned in the space allocated. Choices are: Centered, Right Justified, or Left Justified.

Check Box Control

This control asks the user to make a choice. The choice is usually "Check all that apply."

```
┌─────────────────────────────────────────────────────────┐
│ ═       CheckBox                                          │
├─────────────────────────────────────────────────────────┤
│ Name:  cbx_employed                        ┌──────────┐   │
│                                            │    OK    │   │
│                                            └──────────┘   │
│ Text:  none                                ┌──────────┐   │
│                                            │  Cancel  │   │
│ ☒ Visible    ☒ Enabled   ☒ Automatic      └──────────┘   │
│                                            ┌──────────┐   │
│ ☐ Checked    ☐ Three State  ☐ Third State  │  Script  │   │
│                                            └──────────┘   │
│ ☐ Left Text  Border:  3D Lowered  ▼        ┌──────────┐   │
│                                            │   Help   │   │
│                                            └──────────┘   │
└─────────────────────────────────────────────────────────┘
```

Important Attributes

Name: Unique name (for this window) identifying this control

Text: Assigns the text to be displayed along with the check box control

Visible: Is this control visible (as a default)?

Enabled: Is this control accessible to the user (i.e., can the user check or uncheck this control)?

Automatic: Causes the check box to be displayed as checked automatically when the user clicks on it, or unchecked when the user clicks on it again (value True), or forces the user to write the code necessary to check the box or uncheck the box when clicked (value False).

Checked: When this control is displayed in its default state, is the box checked (value True) or unchecked (value False)?

Three State: The normal state for a check box is either on or off (True or False); Three State says that there may be a third valid state for this check box

Third State: If Three State is chosen, this is where the third state is described

LeftText: Displays the caption (text) associated with the check box to the left of the check box (value True) or to the right of the check box (value False)

Border: Chooses the border for the control

Command Button Control

This control is used to perform an action.

```
┌──────────────────────────────────────────────────────────────┐
│ ▬                    CommandButton                             │
├──────────────────────────────────────────────────────────────┤
│                                                                │
│  N̲ame:  ┌──────────────────────────────┐    ┌──────────────┐  │
│         │cb_print                      │    │     OK       │  │
│         └──────────────────────────────┘    └──────────────┘  │
│                                              ┌──────────────┐  │
│  T̲ext:  ┌──────────────────────────────┐    │   Cancel     │  │
│         │none                          │    └──────────────┘  │
│         └──────────────────────────────┘    ┌──────────────┐  │
│                                              │   S̲cript     │  │
│   ☒ V̲isible   ☒ E̲nabled   ☐ D̲efault  ☐ C̲ancel └──────────────┘  │
│                                              ┌──────────────┐  │
│                                              │    Help      │  │
│                                              └──────────────┘  │
└──────────────────────────────────────────────────────────────┘
```

Important Attributes

Name: Unique name (for this window) identifying this control

Text: Assigns the text to be displayed along with the push-button control

Visible: Is this control visible (as a default)?

Enabled: Is this control accessible to the user (i.e., can the user click on this control)?

Default: Activate this pushbutton as the default action (value True), or make this button just another pushbutton (value False). If this button is the default action button, it will receive the clicked event when the user simply presses enter, choosing any other action.

Cancel: Indicates whether this button will act as the window cancel button (i.e., cancels any changes you have made and exits the window)

Radio Button Control

This control is used to ask the user to make a choice. The choice is usually "Choose one of the choices listed."

RadioButton			
Name:	rb_gender		**OK**
Text:	none		**Cancel**
☒ **Visible**	☒ **Enabled**	☒ **Automatic**	**Script**
☐ **Left Text**	☐ **Checked**	**Border:** 3D Lowered ▼	**Help**

Important Attributes

Name: Unique name (for this window) identifying this control

Text: Assigns the text to be displayed along with the radio button control

Visible: Is this control visible (as a default)?

Enabled: Is this control accessible to the user (i.e., can the user click on this control)?

Automatic: Causes the radio button to be displayed as checked automatically when the user clicks on it, or unchecked when the user clicks on it again (value True); or forces the user to write the code necessary to check the box or uncheck the radio button when clicked (value False)

LeftText: Displays the caption (text) associated with the radio button to the left of the radio button (value True) or to the right of the radio button (value False)

Checked: When this control is displayed in its default state, is the radio button is checked (value True) or unchecked (value False)?

Border: Chooses the border for the control

Group Box Control

This control is used to group controls together: It builds a logical relationship between the controls within the group box.

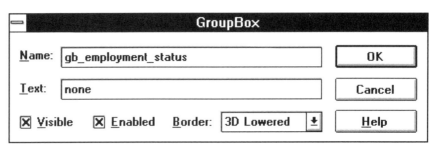

Important Attributes

Name: Unique name (for this window) identifying this control

Text: Assigns the text to be displayed with the group box control

Visible: Is this control visible (as a default)?

Enabled: Is this control accessible to the user (i.e., can the user click on the group box)?

Border: Chooses the border for the control

Single Line Edit Control

This control is used to collect a single line of text; it is typically used as an input field.

```
┌─────────────────────────────────────────────────────────────┐
│ ▬                          SingleLineEdit                     │
├─────────────────────────────────────────────────────────────┤
│  N̲ame:  ┌──────────────────────────────────┐   ┌───────────┐ │
│         │ sle_employee_name                │   │    OK     │ │
│         └──────────────────────────────────┘   └───────────┘ │
│  T̲ext:  ┌──────────────────────────────────┐   ┌───────────┐ │
│         │                                  │   │  Cancel   │ │
│         └──────────────────────────────────┘   └───────────┘ │
│  ☒ V̲isible      ☒ E̲nabled      ☐ P̲assword     ┌───────────┐ │
│                                                │  S̲cript   │ │
│  ☐ Au̲to HScroll    ☐ D̲isplay Only             └───────────┘ │
│                                                ┌───────────┐ │
│  A̲ccelerator: ┌────┐   C̲ase:  ┌──────────┬─┐  │   H̲elp    │ │
│               └────┘          │ Any      │±│  └───────────┘ │
│  L̲imit:  ┌────┐       B̲order: ┌──────────┬─┐                │
│          │  0 │               │3D Lowered│±│                │
│          └────┘               └──────────┴─┘                │
└─────────────────────────────────────────────────────────────┘
```

Important Attributes

Name: Unique name (for this window) identifying this control

Text: Initial text assigned to the single line edit field as a default

Visible: Is this control visible (as a default)?

Enabled: Is this control accessible to the user (i.e., can the user enter data in this entry field)?

Password: Determines whether the single line edit field is a password (asterisks appear when the user types in data (value True)) or not (value False)

Auto Horizontal Scroll: Determines if the control will have a horizontal scroll bar active when data is added or deleted

DisplayOnly: Determines whether the user can change the data (value False) or not (value True)

Accelerator: The value of the key (in ASCII) that acts as the accelerator key (underlined characters; for example, File) for this field

Case: Chooses the case display characteristics for data, once entered—values are AnyCase, Lower, or Upper

Limit: Specifies the maximum number of characters the single line edit control will allow; values are 0 to 32767, where 0 means unlimited

Border: Chooses the border for the control

Multi Line Edit Control

This control is used to collect (or edit) multiple lines of text. Typically used as an input field.

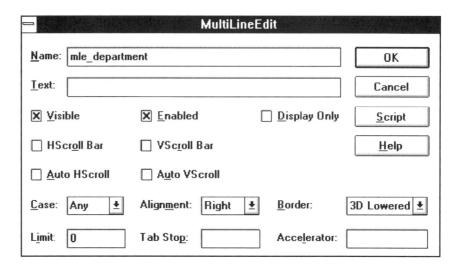

Important Attributes

Name: Unique name (for this window) identifying this control

Text: Initial text assigned to the multiline edit field as a default

Visible: Is this control visible (as a default)?

Enabled: Is this control accessible to the user (i.e., can the user enter data in this entry field)?

DisplayOnly: Determines whether the user can change the data (value False) or not (value True)

Horizontal Scroll Bar: Determines if the control will always have a horizontal scroll bar active (value True) or not (value False)

Vertical Scroll Bar: Determines if the control will always have a vertical scroll bar active (value True) or not (value False)

Auto Horizontal Scroll: Determines if the control will have a horizontal scroll bar active when data is added or deleted

Auto Vertical Scroll: Determines if the control will have a vertical scroll bar active when data is added or deleted

Case: Chooses the case display characteristics for data, once entered—values are AnyCase, Lower, or Upper

Alignment: How the text is aligned in the space provided

Border: Chooses the border for the control

Limit: Specifies the maximum number of characters the multiline edit control will allow; values are 0 to 32767, where 0 means unlimited

Tab Stop: Specifies if and where tab stops will be located

Accelerator: The value of the key (in ASCII) that acts as the accelerator key (underlined characters; for example, File) for this field

Dropdown List Box Control

This control is used to make a choice from a static or dynamic list. The control is actually a combination of a list box (a static set of choices) and a single line edit field. Its attributes determine its flexibility—the control can be designed to allow the user only a given selection or to type in his or her own choice.

DropDownListBox

<u>N</u>ame: `ddlb_state_codes`	OK
<u>T</u>ext: `[                    ]`	Cancel
☒ <u>V</u>isible ☒ <u>E</u>nabled ☐ <u>A</u>llow Editing	Script
☒ Sorte<u>d</u> ☐ Always Sh<u>ow</u> List ☐ A<u>u</u>to HScroll	Help
☒ VScroll <u>B</u>ar Bo<u>r</u>der: `3D Lowered ±`	
<u>L</u>imit: `0` A<u>c</u>celerator: `[  ]`	
<u>I</u>tems: `[                    ]`	

Important Attributes

Name: Unique name (for this window) identifying this control

Text: Initial text assigned to the drop down list box edit field as a default

Visible: Is this control visible (as a default)?

Enabled: Is this control accessible to the user (i.e., can the use enter data in this entry field)?

AllowEditing: Allows the user to enter or edit the text in the single line edit part of the drop down list box

Sorted: Sorts the list box entries in ascending order (value True) or displays them as is (value False)

AlwaysShowList: Always displays the option list (value True), or only displays the option list when the user clicks on the down arrow (value False)

Auto Horizontal Scroll: Determines if the control will have a horizontal scroll bar active when data is added or deleted

Vertical Scroll Bar: Determines if the control will always have a vertical scroll bar active (value True) or not (value False)

Border: Chooses the border for the control

Limit: Specifies the maximum number of characters the drop down list box control will allow; values are 0 to 32767, where 0 means unlimited

Accelerator: The value of the key (in ASCII) that acts as the accelerator key (underlined characters; for example, File) for this field

Items: Contains the list of items to be displayed as choices in the drop down list box as the default

List Box Control

This control is used to make a choice from a static or dynamic list.

```
┌──────────────────────────────────────────────────────────────┐
│ ▬                        ListBox                               │
├──────────────────────────────────────────────────────────────┤
│ Name:  lb_account_numbers                      ┌──────────┐    │
│                                                │    OK    │    │
│ ☒ Visible      ☒ Enabled      ☒ Sorted         └──────────┘    │
│                                                ┌──────────┐    │
│ ☐ HScroll Bar  ☒ VScroll Bar  ☐ Multiple Selections│ Cancel │ │
│                                                ┌──────────┐    │
│ Tabs: [     ]   Accelerator:[  ]  Border: 3D Lowered│ Script │ │
│                                                ┌──────────┐    │
│ Items: ┌──────────────────────────────────┐↑  │   Help   │    │
│        │                                  │   └──────────┘    │
│        │                                  │                   │
│        │                                  │                   │
│        │                                  │↓                  │
│        └──────────────────────────────────┘                   │
└──────────────────────────────────────────────────────────────┘
```

Important Attributes

Name: Unique name (for this window) identifying this control

Visible: Is this control visible (as a default)?

Enabled: Is this control accessible to the user (i.e., can the user select any listed item)?

Sorted: Sorts the list box entries in ascending order (value True) or displays them as is (value False)

Horizontal Scroll Bar: Determines if the control will always have a horizontal scroll bar active (value True) or not (value False)

Vertical Scroll Bar: Determines if the control will always have a vertical scroll bar active (value True) or not (value False)

Multiple Selections: Allows the user to make multiple selections (value True) or not (value False)

Tabs: Indicates if tabs are available

Accelerator: The value of the key (in ASCII) that acts as the accelerator key (underlined characters; for example, File) for this field

Border: Chooses a border for the control

Items: Contains the list of items to be displayed as choices in the drop down list box as the default

DataWindow Control

A DataWindow is a special, powerful control that allows you to show and manipulate data from a relational DBMS without having to code SQL scripts. A DataWindow is created in the DataWindow painter and stored in a library for use. Use this icon to place a DataWindow on the screen and define its general display attributes, then link the display DataWindow control with the DataWindow specifics stored in the library.

A pop-up window will be displayed asking you which Data-Window from which library you wish to connect to this window object.

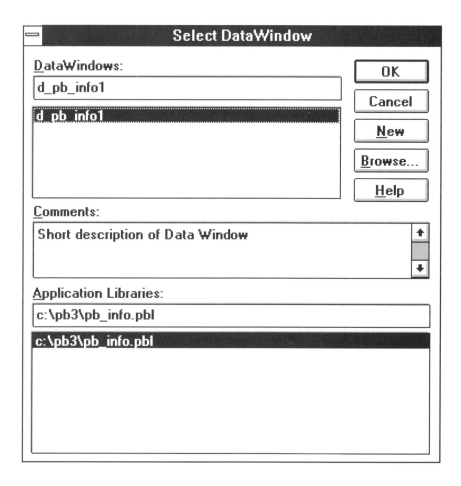

```
┌─────────────────────────────────────────────────────────────┐
│ ▭              DataWindow - d_pb_info1                        │
├─────────────────────────────────────────────────────────────┤
│  N̲ame:  ┌──────────────────────────────────────┐  ┌────────┐ │
│         │ dw_list_account_numbers              │  │   OK   │ │
│         └──────────────────────────────────────┘  └────────┘ │
│  T̲itle: ┌──────────────────────────────────────┐             │
│         │                                      │  ┌────────┐ │
│         └──────────────────────────────────────┘  │ Cancel │ │
│  ☒ V̲isible    ☒ E̲nabled    ☐ Title B̲ar         └────────┘ │
│                                                   ┌────────┐ │
│  ☐ Control Men̲u  ☐ Maximi̲ze Box  ☐ Mi̲nimize Box │ S̲cript │ │
│                                                   └────────┘ │
│                                                   ┌────────┐ │
│  ☐ R̲esizable  ☐ HScro̲ll Bar  ☐ VScro̲ll Bar      │ C̲hange…│ │
│                                                   └────────┘ │
│  ☒ Live Scrolling ☐ H Sp̲lit Scrolling  B̲order:┌─────┐┌──┐ ┌────────┐│
│                                         │ Box ││ ↓│ │  H̲elp  ││
│                                         └─────┘└──┘ └────────┘│
└─────────────────────────────────────────────────────────────┘
```

An attribute window will be displayed allowing you to define the attributes associated with the display of this DataWindow.

Important Attributes

Name: Unique name (for this window) identifying this control

Title: The title associated with the DataWindow

Visible: Is this control visible (as a default)?

Enabled: Is this control accessible to the user (i.e., can the user enter data in this DataWindow)?

TitleBar: Determines if the DataWindow has a title bar—if the DataWindow has a title bar, it can also have maximize, minimize, and control menu boxes.

Maximize: Option only pertinent if the DataWindow has a title bar; this allows the DataWindow to have a maximize box on the title bar, and gives the user the ability to make the DataWindow display full screen

Minimized: Option only pertinent if the DataWindow has a title bar; this allows the DataWindow to have a minimize box on the title bar, and gives the user the ability to make the DataWindow display as an icon on the screen

Control Menu: Option only pertinent if the DataWindow has a title bar; determines if the DataWindow has a control menu box on the title bar. If the control menu box is active, it will contain the standard choices (Close, Maximize, Minimize, Move, Size, Restore, Size and Switch To)

Resizable: If this attribute is turned on, the user can resize the Data Window dynamically

Horizontal Scroll Bar: Determines if the control will always have a horizontal scroll bar active (value True) or not (value False)

Vertical Scroll Bar: Determines if the control will always have a vertical scroll bar active (value True) or not (value False)

LiveScrolling: Determines whether the DataWindow object will move the scroll box

H Split Scrolling: Determines where the horizontal split will occur

Border: Chooses the border for the control

Picture Control

This control is used to display a picture (a bitmap). There are no events for a picture control.

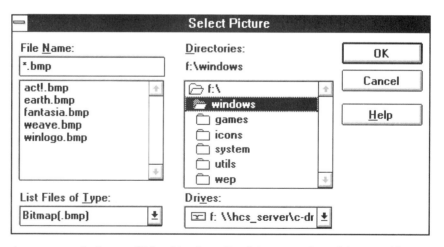

A pop-up window will be displayed asking you for a bitmap (.bmp) picture file to connect with this control. After you have selected the picture, an attribute window will be displayed allowing you to define the attributes associated with the display of this picture.

Picture

Name: | p_season_of_year | OK

File Name: | c:\windows\mvschain.bmp | Cancel

Script

[X] Visible   [X] Enabled   [ ] Focus Rectangle   Change...

[ ] Original Size   [ ] Invert Image   Border: None   Help

Important Attributes

Name: Unique name (for this window) identifying this control

FileName: The name, drive, and location of the bitmap file containing the picture (chosen from the bitmap selection panel)

Visible: Is this control visible (as a default)?

Enabled: Is this control accessible to the user?

Focus Rectangle: Will the dotted rectangle appear on this control when it is in focus?

Original Size: If original size is checked, the picture will be displayed in its original height and width instead of being squeezed into the size you painted with the picture box

Invert Image: Displays the image with its colors as they were painted (value False) or inverted (value True)

Border: Chooses the border for the control

Picture Button Control

This control is a combination picture and command button. As a command button, this control is used to make a decision or turn an option on or off. One of the nice features of this control is that it can display different pictures when the button is depressed or released.

A pop-up window will be displayed asking you for a bitmap (.bmp) picture file to connect with this control. This bitmap will be used when the button is depressed and released, unless you choose a different picture to be displayed when the button is released.

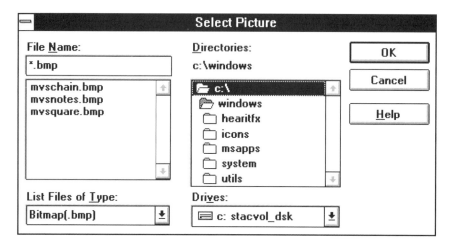

An attribute window will be displayed allowing you to define the attributes associated with the display of this picture.

Important Attributes

Name: Unique name (for this window) identifying this control

Text: The text to be associated with this control

Enabled File: This is the drive, path, filename of the bitmap to be used in the picture button. If there is no disabled file name specified, this picture will be used whether the button is depressed or released. To change this field, you can press the Change Enabled button to get a Select Picture popup box

Disabled File: This is the drive, path, filename of the bitmap to be used in the picture button when the button is depressed. This attribute can be left blank. To change this field, you can press the Change Enabled button to get a Select Picture popup box

Visible: Is this control visible (as a default)?

Enabled: Is this control accessible to the user (i.e., can the user click on this control)?

Original Size: If original size is checked, the picture will be displayed in its original height and width instead of being squeezed into the size you painted with the picture box

Default: Activates this pushbutton as the default action (value True) or makes this button just another pushbutton (value False). If this button is the default action button, it will receive the clicked event when the user simply presses Enter, choosing any other action

Cancel: Indicates whether this button will act as the window cancel button (i.e., cancels any changes you have made and exits the window)

Horizontal Alignment: This attribute determines how the text will be aligned on the picture button; choices are: left, center, and right

Vertical Alignment: This attribute determines how the text will be aligned on the picture button; choices are: Bottom, MultiLine, Top, Vertical Center

Edit Mask Control

This control is used to define the edit mask for a column.

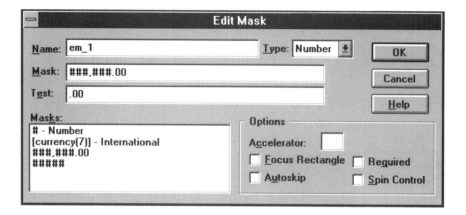

Important Attributes

Name: Unique name (for this window) identifying this control

Mask: The edit mask that has been selected

Test: A sample of what the data will look like after the mask is applied

Masks: A list box of available edit masks to select from

Accelerator: The value of the key (in ASCII) that acts as the accelerator key (underlined characters; for example, File) for this field

Focus Rectangle: Determines if the dotted rectangle will appear when the column has focus

Required: Determines if this is a required column

Autoskip: Determines if this column can be skipped automatically

Spin Control: Determines if the user will be able to scroll through the list of possible values

The Controls menu includes most of the controls which are available from the PainterBar.

CommandButton	Picture
PictureButton	GroupBox
StaticText	UserObject...
SingleLineEdit	Graph
EditMask	Line
MultiLineEdit	Oval
ListBox	Rectangle
CheckBox	RoundRectangle
RadioButton	HScrollBar
DataWindow	VScrollBar
DropDownListBox	

The following controls

> Horizontal Scroll Bar
>
> Vertical Scroll Bar
>
> Rectangle
>
> Line
>
> Oval
>
> Round Rectangle

are accessed from the Controls menu only.

Horizontal Scroll Bar Control

This control is generally used to show a user the percentage of a task that is complete. It is NOT the type of control that usually allows a user to scroll through information.

HScrollBar		
Name: `hsb_percentage_done`		OK
		Cancel
Max Position: `0` **Position:** `0`		Script
Min Position: `0` ☒ **Visible** ☒ **Standard Height**		Help

Important Attributes

Name: Unique name (for this window) identifying this control

Max Position: The maximum number to be set in the position variable when the scroll bar is at its maximum position

Position

Min Position: The minimum number to be set in the position variable when the scroll bar is at its minimum position

Visible: Is this control visible (as a default)?

Standard Height: Use the standard height for a scroll bar (value True) or override with the standard height set for your system

Vertical Scroll Bar Control

This control is generally used to show a user the percentage of a task that is complete. It is NOT the type of control usually used to allow a user to scroll through information.

VScrollBar

Name: vsb_tasks_to_do

Max Position: 0   Position: 0

Min Position: 0   ☒ Visible   ☐ Standard Width

OK

Cancel

Script

Help

Important Attributes

Name: Unique name (for this window) identifying this control

Max Position: The maximum number to be set in the position variable when the scroll bar is at its maximum position

Position

Min Position: The minimum number to be set in the position variable when the scroll bar is at its minimum position

Visible: Is this control visible (as a default)?

Standard Width: Use the standard width for a scroll bar (value True) or override with the standard width set for your system

Rectangle Control

This control is used to draw a rectangle on the window. You can use this control for aesthetic purposes to group controls together without affecting how they operate.

Rectangle	
N̲ame: r_draw_rectangle	OK
	Cancel
☒ V̲isible Line T̲hickness: 5	Help

Important Attributes

Name: Unique name (for this window) identifying this control

Visible: Is this control visible (as a default)?

Line Thickness: The thickness of the line around the box in PowerBuilder units

Line Control

This control is used to draw a straight or dashed line on the window.

Important Attributes

None

Oval Control

This control is used to draw an oval or circular object on the window. You can use this control for aesthetic purposes to group controls together without affecting how they operate.

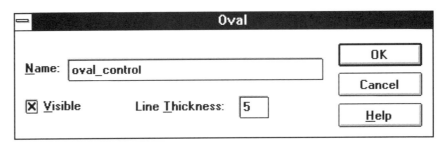

Important Attributes

Name: Unique name (for this window) identifying this control

Visible: Is this control visible (as a default)?

Line Thickness: The thickness of the line around the circle in PowerBuilder units

Round Rectangle Control

This control is used to draw a rectangle with rounded corners on the window. You can use this control for aesthetic purposes to group controls together without affecting how they operate.

Important Attributes

Name: Unique name (for this window) identifying this control

Visible: Is this control visible (as a default)?

Line Thickness: The thickness of the line around the rectangle in PowerBuilder units

Corner Height: The radius of the vertical part of the corners

Corner Width: The radius of the horizontal part of the corners

OTHER WINDOW PAINTER FEATURES

Delete

Use the Delete icon to remove a control. Click on the control to make it active, and click on the Delete icon to remove it.

Script

Use the Script icon to gain access to the script window for the currently active object.

User Object

Use the User Object icon to place a user-defined object on the window. You will be asked to choose a user-defined object (an object you previously created in the User Object Painter) and then you will be allowed to set its attributes.

Run

Use the Run icon to run the application in normal mode.

Debug

Use the Debug icon to run the application under the PowerBuilder debugger.

Selection

Use the Selection icon to cancel selection of a control before it can be placed in a window.

Graph

Use the Graph icon to place a graph on the window.

Off the Design Menu Option

Preview Can be used to preview a window to see how it will look to a user

Window Position Can be used to set the location of the window on the screen when it first comes up

SETTING TAB ORDER

Window Painter sets a default tab value for each control placed in the window, allowing the user to move among controls by pressing the Tab key or the Shift+Tab keys.

To Change the Default Sequence

1. Select Tab Order from the Design menu. You will see a tab value above each control.

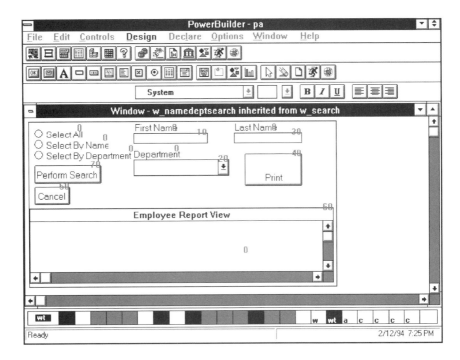

2. With the mouse, select a tab value and change the value.
3. Set tab value to 0 (zero) to prevent the user from tabbing to the control.
4. Select Tab Order to leave the window and confirm that the changes have taken place.
5. Select Tab Order from the Design menu again to save the tab sequence.

   NOTE: Tab increments do not need to be in multiples of 10. However, PowerBuilder will resequence your tab numbers by increments of 10 when you save the tab sequence.

INHERITING WINDOWS

To save coding time, you can build a window that uses the same characteristics as another window. Revise a previously built window, then save it under another name.

Types of Windows

Ancestor Previously built window, menu, or user object

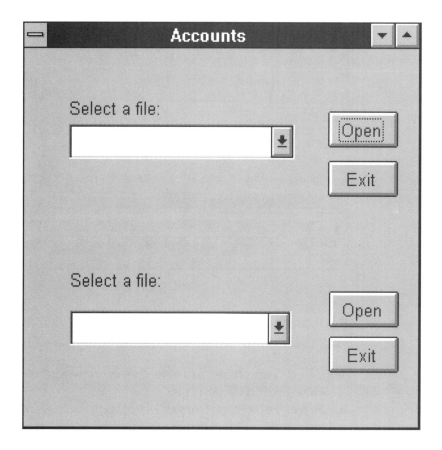

Descendant New window, menu, or user object that inherited its definition from ancestor window, menu, or user object

Inherited Characteristics

- Controls
- Structures
- Events
- Scripts

- Functions
- Attributes

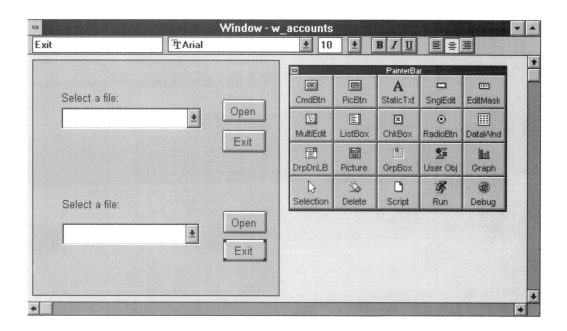

Multiple Descendants When you make changes to ancestor objects, the changes are made automatically in all descendants to that object.

Using Descendant Windows

In the descendant window you can . . .

- Size and position windows and controls
- Reference the ancestor functions, events, and structures
- Declare functions, structures, and variables
- Extend or override inherited scripts
- Declare user events for the window and its controls
- Change attributes
- Add controls and modify controls
- Build new scripts for events

In the descendant window you cannot . . .

* Delete inherited controls (if an inherited control is not needed, you can make it invisible)

Building a Descendant Window

1. Select Inherit from the File Menu Option.

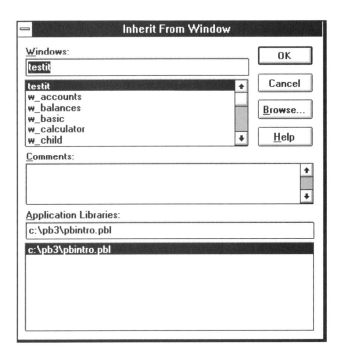

2. Choose the ancestor window you want to use. Click on OK.
3. Make your changes to characteristics, move controls or add new controls.
4. Save your new window using a new name.

PowerBuilder Menu Painter

This chapter explains the capabilities of the PowerBuilder Menu Painter, which is used to build menus that are not created from existing menus. Menus provide users an easy, intuitive way to select commands and options in applications. Various types of menus are used in PowerBuilder and described in this chapter. You will also learn to differentiate between pulldown menus and cascading menus, and you will work with scripts, accelerator keys and shortcut keys.

POWERBUILDER MENU PAINTER

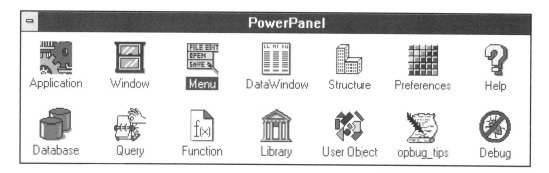

A menu is a list of available options or actions a user can select and perform in the current window. Actions or options are usually related to one menu leg. Menu Painter is used to specify the choices displayed in the menu bar (the menu across the top of the window), the choices available under each menu bar item, and the display style for the choices.

MENU TYPES

Menu Bar

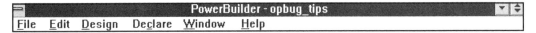

The Menu Bar contains a list of pulldown menus available for the window.

Pulldown Menus

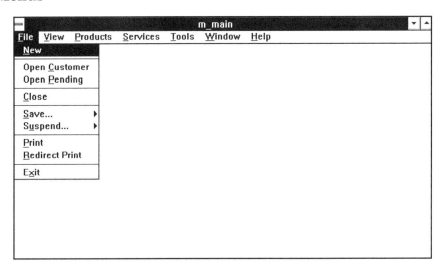

CUA Standards

Every window should have a File, Edit, and Help pulldown.

Each menu option should have an accelerator key (one letter of the menu selection which is underlined. A menu item can be activated by clicking on the menu choice or by pressing the ALT key and the accelerator key—the underlined letter). An accelerator key is designated by placing an ampersand (&) before the key in the menu item you wish to use for the Accelerator Key. For example, defining a File pulldown menu as &File will produce the visual text File and make ALT + F the key combination used to activate the File pulldown menu.

A menu item may have a shortcut key. A shortcut key is a CTRL, SHIFT, and/or ALT plus another key combination that can activate the menu selection. For example, CTRL + F4 may be used to activate the Close menu selection.

Logical menu selections should be separated by menu separators (i.e., a solid line _____). A solid line can be created in a menu by using a single hyphen (-) as the menu item text.

Any menu item which activates another window should end in an ellipsis (. . .).

Cascading Menus

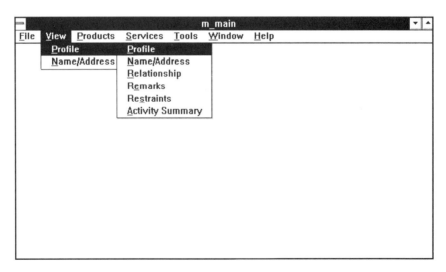

A menu item may have a cascading menu (a menu hanging off a menu). A menu item which has a cascading menu has a triangle to the right of the menu text.

CREATING/MODIFYING MENUS

Click on the Menu painter icon on the power panel. The Menu Painter will display the Select Menu window.

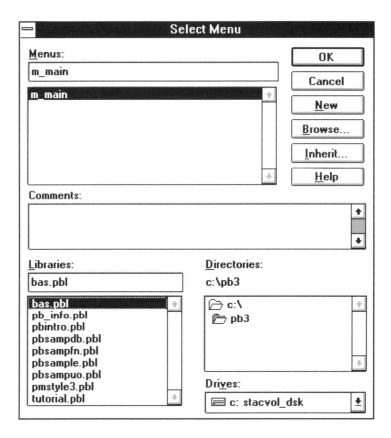

From the top list, choose the name of the existing menu you wish to work with, or click on New to work with a new menu.

Other Options

Click on the Browse button to search existing menus for a text string.

Click on the Inherit button to choose an existing menu to

inherit from. Remember, inherit means to start with a menu with the same characteristics (and scripts) as an existing menu. Existing menu items and attributes can be overridden but a menu choice inherited from an ancestor cannot be deleted.

Note: When working with a new or inherited menu, we suggest you choose Save As from the file menu and save the new menu with a specific name.

THE MENU PAINTER

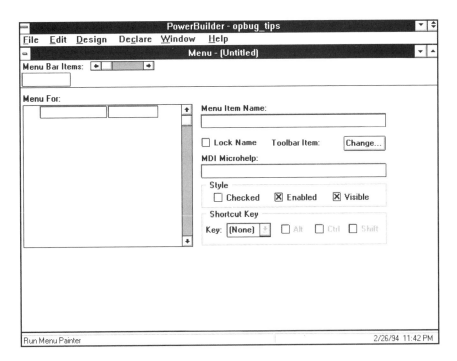

Menu Painter PainterBar

The controls on the Menu Painter Painter Bar are:

Insert: Allows the developer to insert a new item on the menu

Move: Allows the developer to change the order of the items on the menu

Delete: Allows the developer to delete an item from the menu

NextLvl: Displays the next level in a cascading menu

PriorLvl: Displays the previous level in a drop down or cascading menu

Script: Opens the script painter to attach a script to the menu

Run: Runs the menu in regular mode

Debug: Runs the menu in debug mode

Working with the Menu Painter

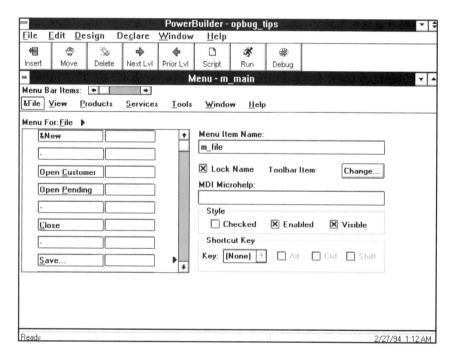

The Menu Bar Items horizontal scroll bar is used to scroll between the menu names available from the menu bar on the open

window. In the picture above, we are currently working with the m_main pulldown.

The items listed in the box underneath Menu For: contains the various options available underneath the menu bar option highlighted. The column on the left is the menu item text; the column on the right is the shortcut key chosen. In the picture above, we are looking at the various menu options available off the m_main pulldown menu.

Use the style box to set menu defaults for each menu item. A menu can be Enabled or Disabled (available or unavailable to the user), Visible or Invisible, and Checked or Unchecked initially.

Use the shortcut key box to choose a shortcut key combination for the menu item highlighted.

Each menu option must have a menu item name (even separator bars). Each name is unique.

To view your work, use the Preview option off the Design pulldown menu (or press CTRL + W).

Use the Save or Save As options under the File pulldown menu to save your work.

1. To access the Menu painter, click on the Menu painter icon either from the PowerBar or the PowerPanel.

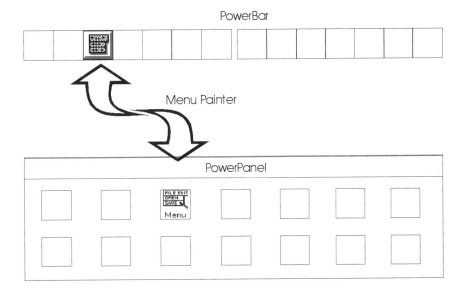

The Select Menu window is presented.

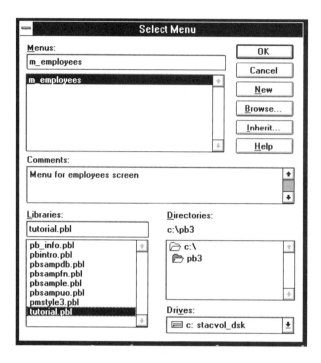

2. Click on New, and the Menu painter workspace is presented.

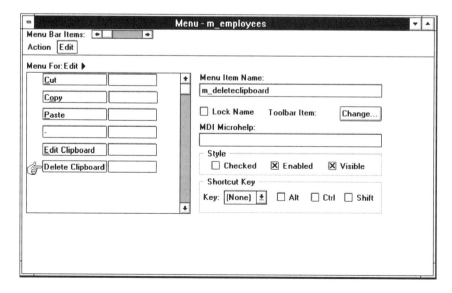

From this screen:

a. Name each item that appears under the menu bar items
b. Name the items that will appear on the action bar
c. Assign a shortcut key, quick-pick key, and/or separator lines to the menu item
d. Establish an MDI microhelp line
e. Modify the display attributes (style) of the MenuItems

Naming MenuItems By default, PowerBuilder assigns a name to any MenuItem added. If that name has already been used, PowerBuilder will suggest another original name for that Menu-Item. MenuItem names lock so accidental changes cannot be made. You can change the text in a MenuItem without changing the name. Also, you can unlock the name if you want it to change when you change the text.

Shortcut Keys Alphabetic keys can be assigned to menu items alone or in combination with the CTRL, SHIFT, or ALT keys.

F1-F12	Del	Ins
CTRL F1-F12	CTRL Del	CTRL Ins
SHIFT F1-F12	SHIFT Del	SHIFT Ins
ALT F1-F12	ALT Del	ALT Ins

Quick-Pick Keys Type an ampersand (&) before the letter in the MenuItem that you want to specify as the accelerator key. The accelerator key will display with an underline under the chosen letter. Users can press ALT + the underlined letter to select that item.

> **EXAMPLE:**
> &Edit
>   &Cut
>   &Copy
>   &Paste
>   &Edit Clipboard
>   &Delete Clipboard

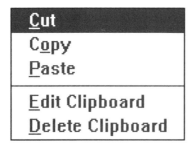

Create Separator Lines You should divide groups of MenuItems with separator lines. To create a separator line type a hyphen (-) as the MenuItem text.

EXAMPLE:

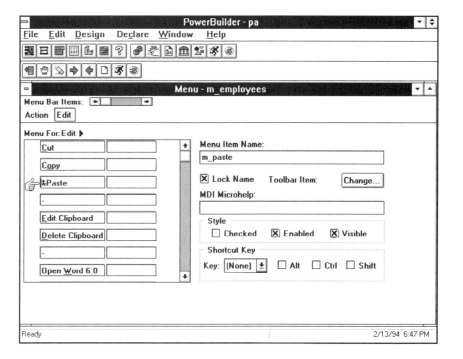

DISPLAYED AS:

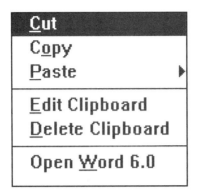

Create a Cascading Menu

1. From the Menu painter, click on the MenuItem you want to build into a cascading menu.

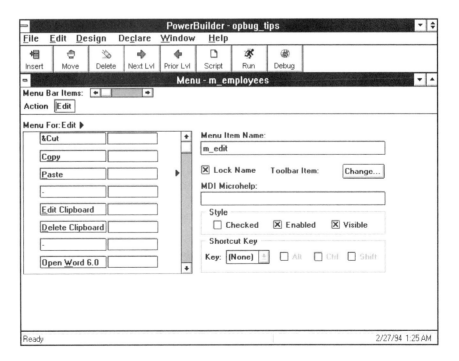

2. Click on Next Level icon from the Edit menu. An empty box is presented under Menu For: for you to build the cascading menu.
3. Type the text that will display for the MenuItem.

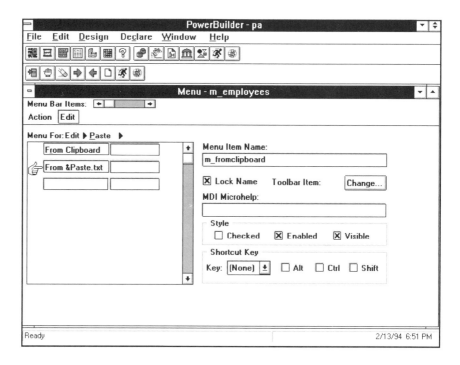

DISPLAYED AS:

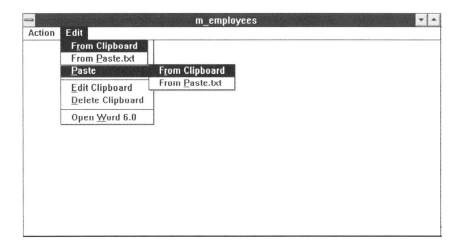

Menu Scripts A script is created for an event in MenuItems. Scripts determine how an item reacts; this action happens when a MenuItem is selected. Use the Fully Qualified Name plus the window name to refer to window controls.

EXAMPLE:
w_employees.sle_status.text="H"

ParentWindow ParentWindow refers to the window in which a menu is used. It can also refer to the attributes of that window, but not to the controls.

Writing a Script The following is the script for the &Close menu item.

1. You write a script for a particular menu item by clicking on the script icon
2. Type: Close(ParentWindow)

3. Click on return to get to the Menu, the script compiles and is
ready to execute

When the correct menu item is selected from the ParentWindow
by the hand indicator, the close script executes.

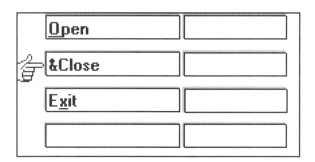

Using a Menu in a Window To see a menu bar when a window
is opened, you relate a menu to the window in the Window painter.

1. Open the window in the Window painter.
2. Select Window Style from the Design menu, or double-click in
the window's background.
3. Click on the Menu checkbox.
4. To the right of the Menu checkbox, a dropdown listbox appears. Select the name of the Menu object.

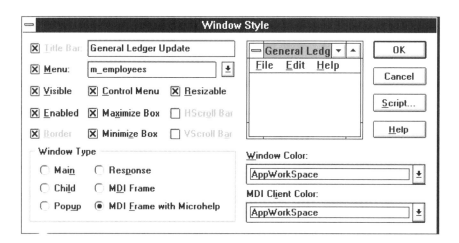

5. To close the Window Style window, click on OK or Script.

The screen print below shows the result of attaching the m_employees menu to the w_main window.

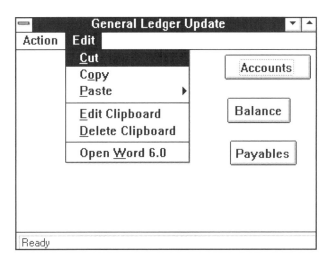

Toolbar Icons You can create a Toolbar of menu items, with each action represented by an icon, by following the procedure below:

1. For the menu item you want to add to the Toolbar, make sure the hand pointer is next to the desired menu item and click the Change button. The screen below will be displayed. This is the Toolbar icon screen.

2. Identify an icon, which must be a *.bmp, to be associated with this menu item. You may also associate an icon to be displayed (Down Picture) when this icon is clicked by the user.

3. The screen below is what the user would see when icons have been associated with the Edit menu items.

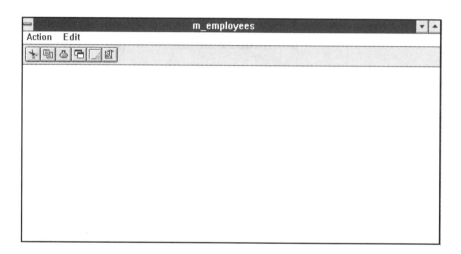

9

PowerBuilder PowerScript

The PowerBuilder language is PowerScript. PowerScript provides a generous array of built-in functions that will execute the objects and controls in your application. In this chapter you will learn how to use the PowerScript painter. You will understand the PowerScript language elements, operators, and expressions. There are four variable scopes that PowerBuilder supports. We will discuss what these are and how they are used. In addition, you will learn how to write a PowerScript, how to change control attributes, and what various functions are associated with PowerScript.

POWERBUILDER POWERSCRIPT: WHAT IS IT?

What Is a Script? A script is a program or series of instructions that defines what actions take place when a particular event occurs for a control. A program in PowerBuilder is written in PowerScript, which is a powerful, BASIC-like language. Scripts cause actions to occur within an application by using the following tools:

Write standard PowerScript statements that control the flow of program operations

Manipulate the attributes of a control (for example, manipulate a controls enable or visible attribute to enable/disable the control or make the control invisible/visible)

Call programmer-written and PowerBuilder functions to perform subroutines

Use SQL statements to perform data access

When and How Is a Script Executed? A script can be coded to respond to an event. When the user performs an action on a control, it causes an event to occur. Whatever script was coded for that event is then executed. When an event is executed, PowerBuilder transfers control to the PowerScript written for that event. If no script was written for the occurring event, PowerBuilder performs the default action (usually nothing).

How Do You Write a PowerScript to Respond to a Particular Event for a Particular Control? Highlight a control in the Window Painter and click on the script icon, or double-click on a control to bring up the attribute window for that control. Then click on the Script pushbutton. Another option is to highlight a control in the Window painter and choose Script off the Edit pulldown menu.

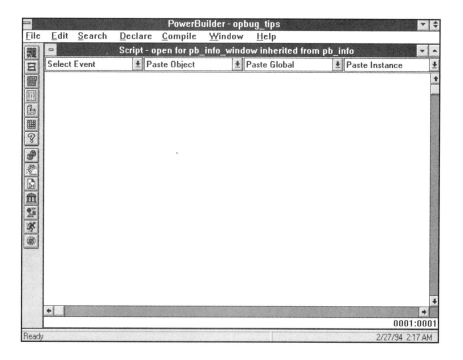

Select Event: Provides a list of events the control you are working with is able to respond to. Each event with a script coded for it will have a Script painter icon next to its name in the list of available scripts.

Paste Object: Provides a list of other controls on this window. When you choose one, the scripting facility simply pastes the name you chose at the current cursor location.

Paste Global: Provides a list of global variables defined for this application. When you choose one, the scripting facility pastes the name you chose at the current cursor location.

Paste Instance: Provides a list of instance and shared variables defined for this application. When you choose one, the scripting facility pastes the name you chose at the current cursor location.

THE SCRIPT PAINTER TOOLBAR

The Painter Bar (Toolbar) is used to select options for creating your script. All of the icons should be relatively self-explanatory.

Note: Try pressing the Paste Statement icon on the toolbar. You will receive the following window:

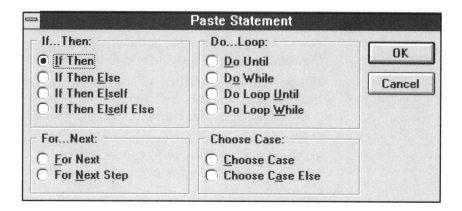

Paste Statement will paste the shell for any of the above statements into your code. If you forget the format of a decision statement, use Paste Statement.

POWERSCRIPT LANGUAGE ELEMENTS

Language Format and the PowerBuilder Compiler

Coding Coding is freeform. The compiler ignores blanks, tabs, formfeeds, and comments (unless it is part of a string). A carriage return is NOT ignored.

Examples:

```
Hours = Minutes * 60
```

The above statement is perfectly acceptable.

```
Hours = Minutes
     * 60
```

The above statement will generate an error.

Comments (//) or (/* */) Comments can be placed within Power-Script code to document what the code is doing and why. Comments can also be used to temporarily remove statements from active execution without deleting them from the script. There are two ways to create a comment: Double slashes (//) and slash asterisk, asterisk slash (/* */).

PowerBuilder allows comments within comments. The double slashes method allows you to create a comment that goes from the beginning of the double slashes to the end of the line.

Examples:

```
Count = Count + 1     //Increment the variable Count
```

The above line has a legal comment in it. The first half of the line is a legal PowerScript statement. The second half is a legal comment.

```
// Count = Count + 1 // Increment the variable Count
```

The above line is also legal.

The slash asterisk, asterisk slash method allows you to enclose a section of code within comment boundaries so the compiler will ignore it.

Examples:

```
Count = Count + 1  /* Comment */
/* Count = Count + 1     /* Comment */ */
```

Both of the above lines are legal examples of commented code.

Continuation Characters (&) Using PowerScript, if you cannot fit a statement on one line or would rather break it up into two lines, you can place a continuation character (an ampersand <&>) on the first line.

Examples:

```
Hours = Minutes
     * 60
```

The above statement will generate an error. However, the statement below will not.

```
Hours = Minutes
       * 60
```

PowerScript Statement Separators (;) In PowerScript, if you choose, you can code multiple statements on a single line. To do this, you must end each statement with a statement separator (a semi-colon <;>) to end each logical statement. For format purposes, some programmers end every statement with a statement separator.

Examples:

```
Count = Count + 1; CountSec = CountSec + 1
```

The above statement is actually two legal statements coded on the same line.

```
Count = Count + 1;
```

The above statement is an example of using the statement separator to signify the end of a statement. It is not required; it is used only for format purposes.

Reserved Words In PowerScript, there are 82 reserved words that cannot be used to name variables, labels, controls, or menu/menu items. For a complete list of reserved words, see the Power-Builder Manuals.

Naming PowerScript Variables, Labels, Controls, Menu, and Menu Items All of the listed objects in PowerScript must be named. An identifier name in PowerScript follows the following rules:

Must be made up of between 1 and 40 characters

Must start with a letter—not a number or special character

Can use the following special characters: (#, $, _, -, %)

Cannot contain spaces

Is case Sensitive (so be cautious)

Code Labels A code label is an identifier placed in a script that is commonly used with a GOTO statement. The format of a label is an identifier followed by a colon (:). Labels can be placed on a line by themselves or on the same line as a valid PowerScript statement.

Examples:

```
Read-Loop: If Count < 30
    or
Read-Loop:
  If Count < 30
```

Special References—Parent, This, and ParentWindow

There will be circumstances where it will be much easier to be able to refer to a control or window by its logical relationship to the current window or control, as opposed to its actual name. For example, there will be times when you will want to refer to the logical relationship in a control's script to effect some kind of change. In fact, it is possible that due to the way an application is written and the way a user chooses to execute, when you write some scripts you may not know the real name of the control you are trying to effect, but you do know the logical relationship.

Parent The keyword Parent is used to reference the window that owns (or is the parent of) the control for which you are writing the script.

Example:

Many windows have pushbuttons for Cancel. You can code the following statement:

```
close(parent)
```

This statement will close the window that owns the control. If the window is a child window, this statement will close both the current window and its parent. More important, the above statement would work *regardless of the name of the parent window*.

ParentWindow   The keyword ParentWindow is used to refer to a controls logical parent window.

Example:
It is often required to effect the attributes of the logical parent window as a result of an interaction with a control. For example, to change the height of a parent window, you can code the following statement:

```
ParentWindow.Height = ParentWindow.Height / 2
```

This statement will cut the height of the parent window in half without actually naming the control parent window.

This   The keyword This is used to refer to the object of the script you are writing. While the keyword This is often not required:

Example:

```
This.enabled = True
   and
enabled = True
```

are equivalent.

The keyword This is often used for documentation purposes only. However, there may be times when a script has a variable which is named the same as an attribute. Under these circumstances, the keyword This is required.

Tilde (~)   The tilde (~) is used to allow you to include certain nonprintable ASCII control characters in a character string. Some common examples are listed below:

Nonprinting Character	Symbol
New Line	~n
Form Feed	~f
Carriage Return	~r
Tab	~t
Vertical Tab	~v
Tilde	~~
Back Space	~b
Quotation Mark	~" or ~'
ASCII Character Code	~nnn (where n is a digit)
Hexadecimal Character Code	~hnn
Octal Character Code	~onn

Examples:

```
"Dear Jim:~n~tPlease Pay Attention"
```

The above string will produce the following output:

```
Dear Jim:
      Please Pay Attention
```

The tilde (~) can also be used to place any character in a string based on its ASCII code.

Null Null is a special value representing a special definition meaning "No Value" or "Not Initialized". If your back-end database supports Null, a null value can be read or written to a variable. The SetNull function can be used to set a variable to Null. The IsNull function can be used to test a variable to see if it is Null.

Examples:

```
int TestInteger
SetNull(TestInteger)
       .
       .
       .
if IsNull(TestInteger) then ...
```

Operators and Expressions

Operator	Meaning	Example	Notes
=	Equals	if A = B then	If A equals B
<	Less Than	if A < B then	If A is less than B
>	Greater Than	if A > B then	If A is greater than B
< >	Not Equal	if A <> B then	If A is not equal to B
< =	Less Than or Equal To	if A <= B then	If A is less than or equal to B
> =	Greater Than or Equal To	if A >= B then	If A is greater than or equal to B

Operator	Meaning	Example	Notes
+	Addition	A = B + C	
-	Subtraction	A = B - C	Spaces Required Around Minus Sign
*	Multiplication	A = B * C	
/	Division	A = B / C	
^	Exponentiation	A = B ^ C	

Operator	Meaning	Example	Notes
+	String Concatenation	A = "Str 1" + "Str 2"	

Operator	Meaning	Example	Note
NOT	Logical Negative	if NOT A = B then . . .	If A is equal to B
AND	Logical Combination	if A = B AND C = D then	If A equals B and C equals D
OR	Logical Exclusion	if A = B OR C = D Then	If A equals B or C equals D

Order of Operator Precedence

```
(), +, -, ^, *, /, =, >, <, <=, >=, <>, NOT, AND, OR
```

As a rule, to control operator precedence, make liberal use of parens <( )> to control precedence.

VARIABLES

Variable Scope

PowerBuilder supports four (4) types of data variable scope: global, shared, instance, local. Global and shared variables are relatively expensive and should be used sparingly.

Note: Global, shared, and instance variables must be declared from the Declare pulldown menu. The Declare pulldown menu exists in the Window painter, PowerScript Window, Menu painter and User Object painter.

Global Variable A global variable is a variable whose scope is across the entire application.

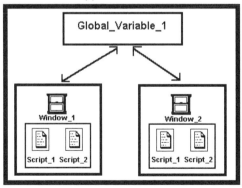

Shared Variable A shared variable is a variable whose scope is across the object where it was defined. It can be defined in an application, menu, window, or user-object. Shared variables retain their value even after the object is closed and reopened;

they also retain their value for each instance of an object. If the value is changed in one instance and then accessed by a second instance, the second instance will get the new value.

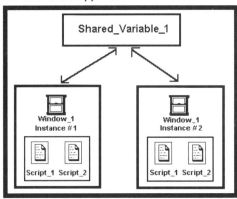

Instance Variables An *application-level* Instance variable can only be used in scripts for the application where it is defined; a *menu-level* Instance variable can only be used in scripts for the menu control where it is defined; a *window-level* Instance variable can only be used'in scripts for the window where it is defined; an *object-level* Instance variable can only be used in scripts for the User Object where it is defined.

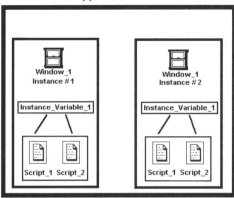

Local Variable A local variable is a variable defined and accessible only in the script for the control where it was defined.

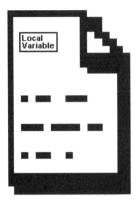

Rules for Variable Declaration

Every variable you use MUST be declared beforehand.

Case is immaterial in datatype name (e.g., INT, Int, and int are all the same).

There must be one space between the data type and variable name.

You can declare more than one variable on a single line (e.g., Int iA, iB, iC). Each variable name must be separated by a comma.

To assign an initial value to a variable other than its default value, use the equal sign (=) right after the definition followed by the value to assign (e.g., int iA = 0).

To Declare a Variable Enter the data type followed by one or more spaces and the variable name to declare a variable.

Format   `data-type<variable-name>{<variable-`
`name>,...}`

To Declare a Decimal Variable Specify the number of digits after the decimal point in braces when declaring a decimal variable.

Default Initial Values PowerBuilder initializes values:

Numeric variables to 0

String variables to the empty string ("")

Date variables to 1900-01-01

DateTime variables to 1900-01-01 00:00:00

Time variables to 00:00:00

Initializing Values Assign alternative initial values (literals only) at the same time that you declare them.

DATA TYPES

PowerBuilder supports the following data types:

String	Real
Boolean	Double
Integer	Date
UnsignedInteger	Time
Long	DateTime
UnsignedLong	Blob
Decimal	

PowerBuilder will also support:

Enumerated Data Types

Arrays

Structures

String

PowerBuilder will support strings of up to 60,000 characters in length. A character in a string can be any valid ASCII character, and a string is generally surrounded by double quotes ("string"). The default is Empty String ("").

Example Definition:

```
string szString1 = "Test";
```

Boolean

A boolean data field is a variable that can only have one of two possible values: True or False. It is very useful as a switch (example: has a condition been met yet; True or False). The default value is False.

Example Definition:

```
boolean bEndOfData = FALSE;
```

Integer

An integer (abbreviated int) is a 16-bit signed integer that has possible values from +32767 to -32768. The default value is 0.

Example Definition:

```
int iCounter = 0;
```

Unsigned Integer

A positive integer (abbreviated unsignedint or uint) is a 16-bit unsigned integer with possible values from 0 to +65,535. The default value is 0.

Example Definition:

```
uint uiCounter = 0;
```

Long

This term signifies a 32-bit unsigned integer with possible values from -2,147,483,648 to +2,147,483,647. The default value is 0.

Example Definition:

```
long lCounter = 0;
```

UnsignedLong

UnsignedLong represents a 32-bit unsigned integer (abbreviated ulong), with possible values from 0 to +4,294,967,295. The default value is 0.

Example Definition:

```
ulong ulCounter = 0;
```

Decimal

Decimal is a signed 32-bit decimal with up to 18 digits (abbreviated dec). Possible values allow for 18 digits with the decimal located in any position. The default value is 0. Decimal is defined using the keyword decimal or dec followed by the number of digits after the decimal point in brackets ({ }).

Example Definition:

```
dec{3} dMultiplier = 0.125;
```

Real

Real is a signed floating point number with up to 6 digits of precision, and possible values between $1.17E^{-38}$ to $3.4E^{+38}$. The default value is 0.

Example Definition:

```
real rMultiplier = 10.125;
```

Double

Double connotes a signed floating point number with up to 15 digits of precision, and possible values between $2.2E^{-308}$ to $1.7E^{+308}$. The default value is 0.

Example Definition:

```
double dblMultiplier = 10.125;
```

Date

This is a formatted date variable with the format: yyyy-mm-dd. The default value is 1900-01-01.

Example Definition:

```
date dateCurrentDate = 1993-07-01;
```

Time

This is a formatted time variable with the format: hh:mm:ss in 24-hour format, and the range 00:00:00 to 23:59:59. The default value is 00:00:00.

Example Definition:

```
date dateCurrentTime = 22:10:21;
```

DateTime

This is an unformatted date and time variable—an internal number that represents the exact date and time. It is used only for reading and writing to a database. See Date(datetime); Time(datetime); datetime(date, time) functions. The default value is 1900-01-0100:00:00.

Example Definition:

```
datetime datetimeCurrentDate = 1993-07-0100:00:00;
```

Blob

This data type is commonly used for storing large quantities of data, for example, pictures or graphics. It can be defined as fixed length (will truncate) or unknown or variable length. Define the data by using the keyword blob followed by the length in brackets ({ }). The default is a zero length (or variable length) blob.

Example Definition:

```
blob blobPicture
```

Declares a blob called blobPicture of unknown length

```
blob{100} blobPicture
```

Declares a blob called blobPicture of fixed (100 bytes) length

ENUMERATED DATA TYPES

Enumerated data types can have a fixed set of values. They are designed to be used as arguments in functions and to specify attributes of an object or control. Examples of choices available for setting the Alignment attribute on a field are:

Alignment	FontCharSet	Pointer
Border	FontFamily	RowFocusInd
Button	FontPitch	SaveAsType
ConvertType	Icon	TextCase
FileMode	LibDirType	WindowStyle
FillPattern		WindowType

Values of enumerated data types always end with an exclamation point (!). They are never enclosed in quotation marks and are not case sensitive.

Alignment	Left!	Icon	Exclamation!
	Center!		Information!
	Right!		StopSign!
			Question!
			None!
Text	Upper!		
	Lower!		
	Anycase!		

ARRAYS

An array is a table or indexable collection of data elements of a single data type. It can be single dimensional or multidimensional: Single dimensional is indexed with a single subscript; multidimensional arrays are indexed with multiple subscripts, one subscript per dimension. Single dimensional arrays can have fixed (predefined) or variable sizes with a maximum of 65,534 elements, and multidimensional arrays must be defined and each dimension or level can have up to 65,534 elements. To declare an array, declare the variable type with the number of elements in each dimension declared within brackets ([ ]). String arrays can hold strings of any size (i.e., the string length does not need to be determined beforehand). Examples of arrays are shown in the following table.

Array Declaration	Explanation	Example Usage
INT Multiplier[3]	Declares a one-dimensional fixed size array with three elements.	ActualMult = Multiplier[2] Assigns second element of the array to the variable
INT Multiplier [3, 6]	Declares a two-dimensional fixed size array with 3 elements in the first dimension and 6 elements in the second dimension.	ActualMult = Multiplier[2, 1] Assigns second element of first dimension, first element of second dimension of the array to the variable
string Names[ ]	Declares a one-dimensional variable-sized array which can hold an undetermined number of strings, each of an undetermined length.	TestString = Names[1] Assigns the first element of the Names array to the variable TestString

Initializing Arrays

Initialize a Single Dimensional Array:

```
INT Multiplier[ ] = {10, 20 ,30}
```

Initializes   Multiplier[1] to 10
Multiplier[2] to 20
Multiplier[3] to 30

Initialize a Two-Dimensional Array:

```
INT Multiplier[3, 2] = { {10,90}, {20, 80}, {30, 70} }
```

Initializes   Multiplier[1, 1] to 10
Multiplier[1, 2] to 90
Multiplier[2, 1] to 20
Multiplier[2, 2] to 80
Multiplier[3, 1] to 30
Multiplier[3, 2] to 70

WRITING SCRIPTS: CHANGING CONTROL ATTRIBUTES IN A SCRIPT

Every control has attributes that determine the way the control is displayed and how it reacts. You can manipulate attributes from within a PowerBuilder script to change a control characteristics "on the fly." You can also test the attributes of a control to determine what action to take. To assign an attribute a value in a script, use the following format:

```
ControlName.Attribute = Value;
```

Example:

```
w_mainwindow.title = "Main Window"
```

Changes the text displayed on the title bar of a window control called mainwindow.

```
w_mainwindow.width = w_mainwindow.width + 4
```

Changes the width of mainwindow from its current size to 4 units larger than the current width.

USING FUNCTIONS IN POWERBUILDER SCRIPT

PowerScript has more than 300 predefined functions. The Function painter can be used to create user-defined functions. Function names are NOT case sensitive, and are written: FunctionName(Argument1, Argument2). A function always has:

A function name

An open parenthesis < (>

Zero, One or More arguments

A close parenthesis <) >

PowerBuilder functions include:

Numeric Functions
String Functions
Date/Time Functions
Type Conversion Functions
File Functions
Print Functions
Other Functions
Control Functions
Window Functions

The next few pages will show some commonly used functions and how they work. Remember: There are over 300 PowerBuilder functions... For a complete reference, see the PowerBuilder Function Reference.

COMMONLY USED FUNCTIONS

Function Tables

Numeric Functions

Function	Datatype Returned	Operation	Example
Int(N)	Returns Datatype of number specified in argument	Returns largest whole number less than or equal to the specified number	Int iResult iResult = Int(12.6) Returns 12
Sign(N)	Returns 1 - Positive 0 - Neutral -1 - Negative	Returns a number indicating the sign of the number requested	Int iResult iResult = Sign(10) Returns 1
Max(X, Y)	Returns the datatype of the variables in question	Returns the larger of the two numbers compared	Int iResult iResult = Max(5, 10) Returns 10
Min(X, Y)	Returns the datatype of the variables in question	Returns the smaller of the two numbers compared	Int iResult iResult = Min(5, 10) Returns 5

Date/Time Functions

Function	Datatype Returned	Operation	Example
Today( )	Date in format yyyy-mm-dd	Returns the current date in yyyy-mm-dd	Date dTodaysDate dTodaysDate = Today( )
RelativeDate (Date, X)	Date in format yyyy-mm-dd	Returns the date that that occurs X days after Date	Date dNewDt dNewDt = RelativeDate (1993-07-01, 15)
DayName (Date)	String - Day Name	Returns Name of Day	String szDay szDay = DayName (1993-07-01)
Now( )	Time in hh:mm:ss format	Returns the current time in hh:mm:ss format	Time tCurrentTime tCurrentTime = Now( )
Time (DateTime)	Returns the time in hh:mm:ss	Returns the time in hh:mm:ss from a DateTime field	Time tTime tTime = Time(dtDateTime)
DateTime (Date,Time)	Returns a DateTime data-type	Takes the time and date given and returns a DateTime	Time tTime Date dDate DateTime dtDateTime tTime = Now( ) dDate = Today( ) dtDateTime = DateTime(tTime,dDate)

String Functions

Function	Datatype Returned	Operation	Example
Fill(String, Length)	String	Returns a string filled with String characters of Length size	String szString szString = Fill("*", 80)
Space(Number)	String	Returns a string filled with spaces of size Number	String szString szString = Space(80)
LeftTrim(String)	String	Returns the String given with leading blanks removed	String szString = " Testing" szString = LeftTrim(szString)
RightTrim(String)	String	Returns the String given with trailing blanks removed	String szString = "Testing " szString = RightTrim(szString)
Len(String)	Unsigned Integer	Returns the length of the given String	String szString = "1234567890" UInt uiLength uiLength = Len(szString)
Lower(String)	String	Returns the given String in lowercase letters	String szString = "AbCdE" szString = Lower(szString)
Upper(String)	String	Returns the given String in uppercase letters	String szString = "AbCdE" szString = Lower(szString)
Match(String, Pattern)	Boolean	Determines if the String passed matches the Pattern given	String szString = "TestString" String szPattern = "[A-Za-z]" Boolean bResult bResult = Match(szString, szPattern)

Type Conversion Functions

Function	Datatype Returned	Operation	Example
Integer(String)	Integer	Returns the contents of String as a number or 0 if cannot be converted	String szString = "12345" Int iNumber iNumber = Integer(szString)
String(Number, Format)	String	Returns the contents of number in the format dictated by Format	String szString szString = String(100, "$#,##0.00)

File/Print Functions

Function	Returned	Operation	Example
FileOpen(FileName, FileMode, FileAccess, FileLock, WriteMode)	Integer - File Handle	Opens the file specified in the mode specified. Returns -1 if open fails	Int iFileHandle iFile = FileOpen("TEST.DAT", LINEMODE!, WRITE!,REPLACE!)
FileRead(FileHandle, Record)	Integer	Reads data off the file opened for the file handle specified. Returns -1 if read fails	String szString Int iResult iResult = FileRead(iFile, szString)
FileWrite(FileHandle, Record)	Integer	Writes data to the file opened for the file handle specified. Returns -1 if write fails	String szString = "Record 1" Int iResult iResult = FileWrite(iFile, szString)
FileClose(FileHandle)	Integer	Returns a 1 if close succeeds, -1 if it fails	Int iResult iResult = FileClose(iFile)
PrintOpen(JobName)	Integer	Returns a -1 if Open fails. Otherwise, returns job number. Opens a job on the print queue with the name given	Int iJob iJob = PrintOpen("Print Job")
Print(JobNumber, String)	Integer	Returns a 1 if print succeeds, -1 if it fails	String szString = "Test Record" Int iResult iResult = Print(iJob, szString)
PrintClose(JobNumber)	Integer	Returns a 1 if close succeeds, -1 if it fails	String szString = "Test Record" iResult = PrintClose (JobNumber)

Other Functions

Function	Returned	Operation	Example
Beep(Number)	Integer - Returns 0	Causes the computer to beep the number of times specified	Int iNumber = 5 Beep(iNumber)
IsDate(String)	Boolean	Checks the string passed to see if it is a valid PowerBuilder Date	IsDate("July 1, 1993")
IsNull (AnyVariable)	Boolean	Checks the variable to see if it contains NULL	String szString = NULL IsNull(szString)
IsNumber (String)	Boolean	Checks the String passed to see if it is numeric	IsNumber("12345")
SetNull (AnyVariable)	Integer	Returns a 1 if succeeds, -1 if fails	String szString SetNull(szString)

Window Functions

Function	Datatype Returned	Operation	Example
Open(Window, WindowName, Parent)	Integer	Returns a 1 if it succeeds, -1 if it fails	Open(W_MainWindow)
Close (WindowName)	Integer	Returns a 1 if it succeeds, -1 if it fails	Close(W_MainWindow)

Structures

A collection of one or more related variables (same or different datatypes) grouped under one name is a structure. A structure will allow you to refer to related objects as a segment rather than individually. You can define a collection of variables as a structure called user_struct then refer to user_struct when needed.

Create a Structure To create a structure you use the Structure painter. Enter the names and datatypes of the variables you want to use in the structure and then name the structure. After creating a structure you can copy it, assign values to it, pass it to functions, and/or have functions return values to it.

To Use a Structure in a Script

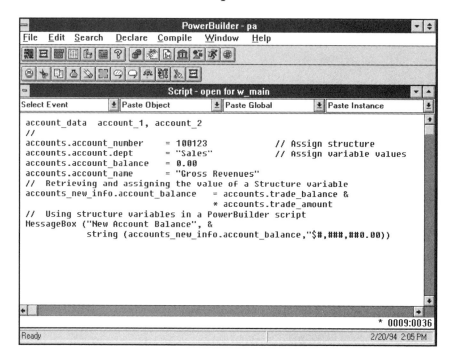

DECISION MAKING IN POWERSCRIPT

IF, THEN, ELSE Statements

The IF, THEN statement is used to make decisions in PowerScript. There are two types of IF, THEN statements: Single and Multiple.

Single IF Statement Format:

```
IF < Expression > THEN < Statement > {ELSE < Statement >}
```

The entire expression must be on one line. Remember: you can use an ampersand (&) to continue a statement.

Multiple IF Statement Format:

```
IF < Expression > THEN
      < Block of Statements >
ELSEIF < Expression > THEN
      < Block of Statements >
ELSE
      < Block of Statements >
END IF
```

Note: END IF required on Multiple IF statement. You can have multiple ELSEIF blocks, but only one END IF is required to end the statement.

Examples:
```
Int iTestVar1 = 0
Int iTestVar2 = 0
/* Single IF, THEN */
IF (iTestVar1 = 0 AND iTestVar2 = 0) THEN
        iResult = 0 ELSE & iResult = 1
/* Multiple IF, THEN */
IF (iResult = 0) THEN
        iTestVar1 = 1
        iTestVar2 = 1
ELSE
        iTestVar1 = 0
        iTestVar2 = 0
END IF
```

Choose Case Statement

Choose Case Statement is used to direct program execution based on the value of a variable.

```
CHOOSE CASE < Expression or Variable >
CASE      < Expression List or Value >
    < Statement Block >
CASE ELSE
    < Statement Block >
END CHOOSE
```

Rules

At least one CASE statement must be coded

< Expression List > can be:
  a single value
  a list of values (separated by commas)
  a range of values (example: 1 TO 3 or IS > 5)
  any combination of the above

When the < Expression or Variable > is equal to the < Expression List or Value >, the statements immediately following the CASE statement are executed.

As soon as a CASE statement is evaluated to True, all statements after the CASE are executed. The next statement executed is the first statement after the END CHOOSE.

If none of the CASE statements evaluates to True, the statements following the CASE ELSE statement will be executed.

Example:

```
Int iTestVar1 = 0
Int iResult

CHOOSE CASE iTestVar1
CASE 0
     iResult = 1
CASE IS>0
     iResult = 2
CASE ELSE
     iResult = 0
END CHOOSE
```

LOOPING IN POWERSCRIPT

Do Statements

The DO statements are used to execute a block of statements continuously. There are four types of DO statements: DO UNTIL, DO WHILE, and LOOP UNTIL, and LOOP WHILE.

DO UNTIL Format:

```
DO UNTIL < Test Condition >
    < Statement Block >
LOOP
```

This expression will cause the statements coded in < Statement Block > to be executed until the condition specified in < Test Condition > is True.

DO WHILE Format:

```
DO WHILE < Test Condition >
    < Statement Block >
LOOP
```

This expression will cause the statements coded in < Statement Block > to be executed while the condition specified in < Test Condition > is True.

LOOP UNTIL Format:

```
DO
    < Statement Block >
LOOP UNTIL < Test Condition >
```

This expression will cause the statements coded in < Statement Block > to be executed until the condition specified in < Test Condition > is True. Note: The < Statement Block > will *always* be executed once.

LOOP WHILE Format:

```
DO
    < Statement Block >
LOOP WHILE < Test Condition >
```

This expression will cause the statements coded in < Statement Block > to be executed while the condition specified in < Test Condition > is True. Note: The < Statement Block > will *always* be executed once.

Examples:

```
Int iCounter = 0
DO UNTIL iCounter > 10
     BEEP(1)
     iCounter = iCounter + 1
LOOP
```

```
DO WHILE iCounter < 20
    BEEP(1)
    iCounter = iCounter + 1
LOOP
DO
    BEEP(1)
    iCounter = iCounter + 1
LOOP UNTIL iCounter > 30
DO
    BEEP(1)
    iCounter = iCounter + 1
LOOP WHILE iCounter < 40
```

FOR, NEXT Statement

The FOR, NEXT statement is used to loop through a block of statements a fixed number of times.

FOR, NEXT Format:

```
FOR <Variable Name> = <Starting Value> TO <Ending Value>
STEP <Increment>
    <Statement Block>
NEXT
```

Rules

STEP is not required. An increment of + 1 is the default.

If the STEP increment is positive, the Ending Value must be greater than the Starting Value.

If the STEP increment is negative, the Ending Value must be less than the Starting Value.

Example:

```
Int iCounter
FOR iCounter = 1 TO 10
    BEEP (iCounter)
NEXT
```

The EXIT Statement

The Exit statement is used to exit out of a DO or FOR, NEXT statement and continue script execution.

Example:

```
Int iCounter
FOR iCounter = 1 TO 10
      iResult = BEEP (iCounter)
      IF iResult = -1 THEN EXIT
NEXT
```

The CONTINUE Statement

The CONTINUE statement is used to skip statement block execution and jump to the next loop.

Example:

```
Int iCounter
Int iBeepsDone
FOR iCounter = 1 TO 10
      iResult = BEEP (iCounter)
      IF iResult = -1 THEN CONTINUE
      iBeepsDone = iBeepsDone + 1
NEXT
```

The RETURN Statement

The RETURN statement is used to exit immediately from a Power-Builder Function or Script.

RETURN Format:

```
RETURN < Value or Expression >
```

Example:

```
IF sle_UserId <> szAcceptablePassword THEN RETURN -1
```

The HALT Statement

The HALT statement is used to exit immediately from a Power-Builder application. There are two choices when coding a HALT statement: HALT with the CLOSE keyword and HALT without the CLOSE keyword. HALT with the CLOSE keyword will exit the application and cause the Close event to be executed. HALT without the CLOSE keyword will simply exit from the application.

Example:

```
IF sle_UserId <> szAcceptablePassword THEN HALT CLOSE
```

The GOTO Statement

The GOTO statement is used to transfer program execution to the first statement following the LABEL given in the statement.

GOTO Format:

```
GOTO < LABEL >
```

Example:

```
GOTO ERROR
 .
 .
 .
ERROR:
 .
 .
 .
```

TRANSACTION OBJECT

All database processing in the PowerBuilder environment uses a transaction object, which identifies specific database connections to PowerBuilder. PowerBuilder creates a default transaction object named SQLCA. You can create other transaction objects. This allows multiple connections to a database or connections to multiple databases.

Transaction Object Data Items

The transaction object contains 14 fields: 10 fields are used for database connection; 4 fields are used for return status information.

Database Connection Fields

Field	Values
DBMS	String containing the name of your DBMS (XDB, Sybase, Gupta)
Database	Name of specific database
UserId	Name of user who will connect
DBPass	Password for database connection
Lock	Isolation level
LogId	User ID to log onto database server
LogPass	Password to log onto server
ServerName	Database server name
Autocommit	True or False
DBparm	Database specific information

The fields above are not applicable to all database vendors; consult your specific PowerBuilder DBMS interface manual for details.

Transaction Object Output Fields

Database Status Fields

Field	Description
SQLCode	Success or failure of SQL command 0 - success 100 - not found -1 - SQL failure
SQLNRows	Number of rows affected by a SQL command
SQLDBCode	Database specific error codes
SQLErrText	Database error message (vendor specific)

CONNECTING TO A DATABASE

SetTransObject Function

```
Syntax: SetTransObject(<datawindow>,<transaction>)
```

where <datawindow> is the name of the DataWindow in which you want to use a programmer-specified transaction object rather than the DataWindow's internal transaction object, and <transaction> is the name of the transaction object you want to use in the DataWindow. The SetTransObject gives the developer control over connection, disconnecting, transaction committing, or rollback. See PowerBuilder manuals for details.

Examples:
This statement causes dw_1 to use the default transaction object SQLCA:

```
SetTransObject(dw_1,SQLCA)
```

This statement causes dw_1 to use the programmer-defined transaction object trans1:

```
SetTransObject(dw_1,trans1)
```

SetTrans Function

```
Syntax: SetTrans(<datawindow>,<transaction>)
```

where <datawindow> is the name of the DataWindow in which you want to set the values of the internal transaction object, and <transaction> is name of the transaction object from which you want the DataWindow to get the values.

Example:
This statement sets the values in the internal transaction object for dw_1 to the values in the default transaction object SQLCA:

```
SetTrans(dw_1,SQLCA)
```

User-Defined Transaction Object

You can create a transaction object using script, or declare a transaction object:

```
Transaction usertran
```

You can also create the transaction object

```
usertran = create transaction
```

and assign values to the transaction object fields

```
usertran.DBMS        = "Sybase"
usertran.database    = "dbtest"
usertran.LogId       = "log1"
usertran.LogPass     = "pass1"
usertran.ServerName  = "fserver"
usertran.Autocommit  = "False"
```

Once the values are assigned you can connect to the database

```
connect using usertran;
```

Note: always check SQLCode after connect, disconnect, commit, rollback. When processing has completed using the user-defined transaction object, you should destroy it to free up resources.

```
Destroy usertran
```

Connect, Disconnect

```
connect <using transobject>
```

Connects to the database; <using transobject> is required when not using the default transaction object SQLCA.

```
disconnect <using transobject>
```

Disconnects from the database; <using transobject> is required when not using the default transaction object SQLCA. Disconnect commits all transactions since the last commit or rollback.

Commit, Rollback

```
Commit <using transobject> ;
```

Permanently updates all database operations since the previous commit, rollback, or connect for the specified transaction object.

Commit does not cause a disconnect, but it closes all cursors associated with the transaction object. <using transobject> is required when not using the default transaction object SQLCA.

```
Rollback <using transobject>
```

Cancels all database operations in the specified database since the last commit, rollback, or connect. Rollback does not cause a disconnect but it does close all cursors associated with the transaction object. <using transobject> is required when not using the default transaction object SQLCA.

FUNCTION PAINTER

To Create a LOCAL Function Access the Function painter from either the PowerScript, Window, Menu, or User Object painter. Click on the Declare menu, and choose the appropriate menuitem: User Object, Application, Window, or Menu functions.

```
Global Variables...
Shared Variables...
Instance Variables...

Window Functions...
Window Structures...

Global External Functions...
Local External Functions...

User Events...
```

To Create a Global Function Create a Global Function from the PowerPanel by double-clicking on the Function painter icon, or click the Function painter icon from the PowerBar.

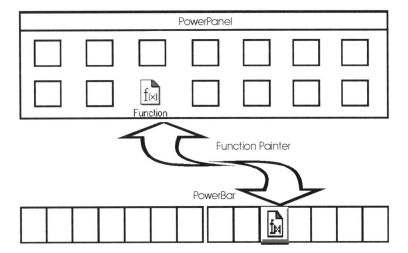

Select Function Window This shows the Select Function window as displayed through the PowerPanel.

Click on New to create a new function or subroutine.

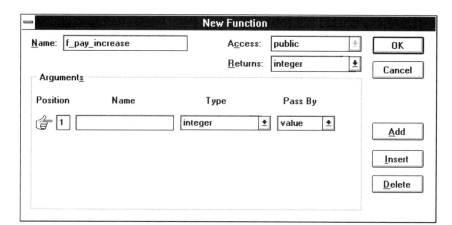

Define a function name, the datatype of the return value, arguments for the function, and type of access.

Define Access to the Function For LOCAL functions, you can decide whether access is public, private, or protected. For GLOBAL functions all access is designated as public, therefore when creating a GLOBAL function the Access box is read-only.

	Public Access	*Private Access*	*Protected Access*
Applies To:	Global and Local Functions	Local Function	Local Function
Can Call From:	Any script in the application	Scripts for events in the object for which the function was defined. You cannot call the function from descendants of the object.	Scripts for the object for which the function was defined and its descendants.
Sample Uses:	Passing values back and forth between a window and a user object.	"Utility Functions" that you call from other functions or scripts within the object.	Calling a function within a descendant object to increase the capabilities of the ancestor object.

Define a Return Type In the Return box, enter a data type. Any PowerBuilder datatype can be used, including standard datatypes: integer and string, or objects and controls—window or MultiLineEdit. You can also use the dropdown list to select a datatype. Since a Subroutine does not return a value to the script that calls it, select None as the Return Type.

Define an Argument User-defined functions can have any number of arguments, including none. Define the arguments and their types when you define a function. Arguments can include:

Objects	Controls
Variables	Arrays

To define an argument

1. Choose a name for the argument.
2. Define the argument type. You can select the datatype from the dropdown list box or you may enter the datatype.
3. Define the method in which the argument is to be passed. By value, you are passing the function a temporary local copy of the argument. The value of the local copy can be altered within the function, but is not changed in the calling script of function. By reference, the function has access to the original argument and can use and change it directly.
4. Click Add after the last argument to add an argument.
5. Place the cursor at the line where you want to insert an argument, click Insert.
6. Place the cursor at the line where you want to delete an argument, click Delete.
7. After entering all arguments, click OK. The New Function window closes and the Function painter workspace displays.

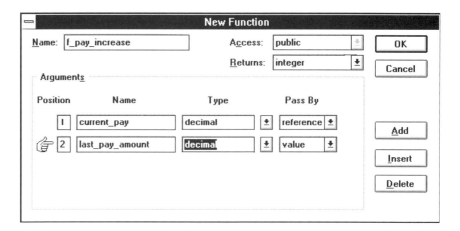

Write the Function After defining the function's name, return type, access level, and arguments from the Function painter, enter the process code that the function executes.

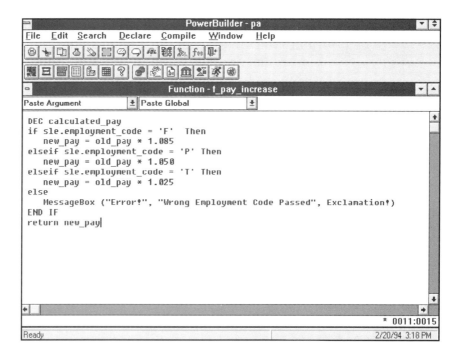

Icons are basically the same in the Function painter as they are in the PowerScript painter.

Pasting Arguments At the top of the Function painter you will see a Paste Arguments DropDownListBox. This box lists the datatypes and arguments defined for the current function or subroutine. To paste an argument into the function, at the insertion point, click on the argument name.

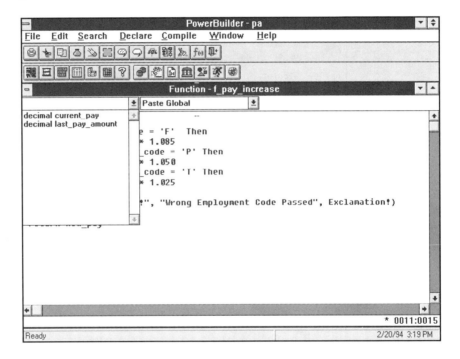

Pasting Global Arguments At the top of the Function painter you will see a Paste Global DropDownListBox. This box lists the global variables defined. To paste a global variable into the function, at the insertion point, click on the global variable name.

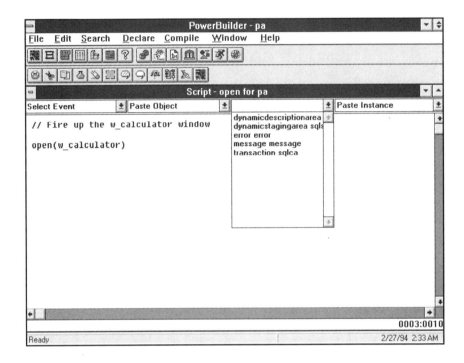

Writing Code Any normal PowerScript code can be used in the function.

Return Value of a Function If you defined a return type for your function, you must return a value to the script that calls it and you must include a Return statement in your function.

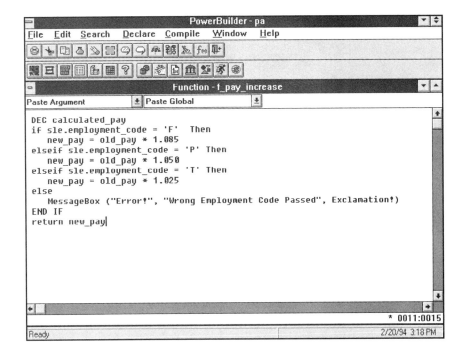

EXAMPLE: RETURN<expression>

Changing a User-Defined Function or Subroutine From the Edit menu on the Function Painter, select Function Declaration.

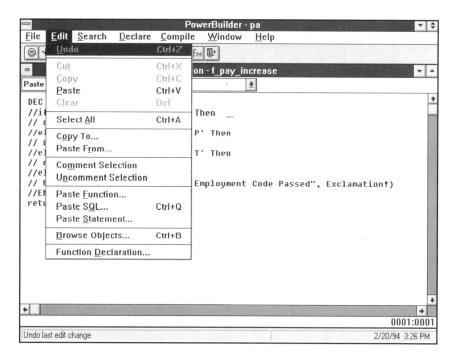

Make your changes, click OK. Save with current name, or choose
Save As and enter a new name.

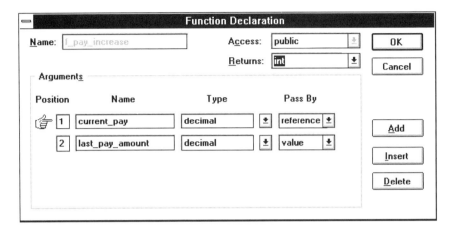

Debugging Your PowerBuilder Application

After you build, compile, and save an application, you can run the application. There are two ways to run an application, in a debug session or in regular mode. After completing this chapter, you will be able to add Edit Stops in a debug session. You will learn what a watch list is, how to work with variables, and how to modify them and their various types.

DEBUG

PowerBuilder's Debug tool allows the PowerBuilder developer to suspend execution of an application at specific points in the script, where the developer may examine or change variables, watch variables, step through code, and/or continue processing.

The typical Debug scenario:

Click on the debug icon on the Power Panel or the Window painter to start the debug session. The first window you will see is the

Debug window. From here you can click on the script you want to debug, set stops in the script, and start the application. Once a program break point is hit, PowerBuilder suspends execution of the application and displays the Debug window. At the Debug window you can:

- Display objects, current values and attributes of the objects, and instance variables
- Display and/or modify the current values of the global, shared, and local variables
- Add/Delete/Modify stops in application script
- Select variables to view during execution in the Watch window
- Step through the script or let the script continue until the next stop

THE DEBUG WINDOW

Icons and Menu Selections

Below is a list of the icons and menu selections in the Debug window.

Start Start the application in debug mode.

Step Step to the next executable PowerScript statement. Step is only available when a stop has been encountered.

Select Script Display the Select Script window and list the scripts in the application.

Edit Display the Edit Stops window and list the current stops.

Show/Hide Watch Open or close the Watch window. The icon acts as a toggle to hide or show the Watch window. The Watch Window allows the developer to watch variables and monitor their current value.

Add Add a variable to the watch list.

Remove Remove variable from watch list.

Show/Hide Variables Display or hide Variable window. This icon acts as a toggle to show or hide the Variable window. The Variable window allows the developer to display global, shared, and local variables.

Menu Items without Icons

Power Panel	Displays the PowerBuilder Power Panel
Printer Setup	Set up printer parameters
Print Variables	Print application variables
Print Watch	Print watch variables

EXECUTING IN DEBUG MODE

The first step in executing is to click on the Debug icon which will bring up the Select Script window. If you had been in debug mode for this application previously and set stops, the Edit Stops window will appear.

Selecting the Application Script to Set Stops

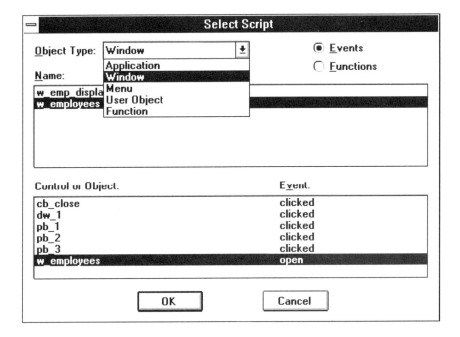

Choose an object type from the Object Type dropdown listbox. Click on the appropriate radiobutton, Events or Functions.

This selection will populate the window labeled Control or Object with either events or user-defined functions.

Click on the name of the specific object from the Name window (this is a list of objects in your application of the type chosen in the Object Type dropdown list box). You are choosing the object to set stops on.

Click on the specific event or function from the window labeled Control or Object.

Note: Do not set stops in scripts for Activate or GetFocus events. These events will occur far too often to debug.

Click on the OK pushbutton and the script you have chosen will be displayed in the Debug window.

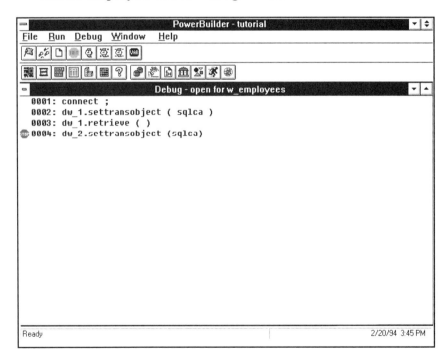

A Stop sign will appear on a line to indicate a stop has been placed at that instruction. This is set by double-clicking on that line. Double-clicking again will remove the stop.

PowerBuilder allows stops to be set only on executable instructions.

If you need to set stops in other scripts, click on the Select Script icon.

Editing Stops

To edit the stops click on the Edit Stops icon. Edit Stops window:

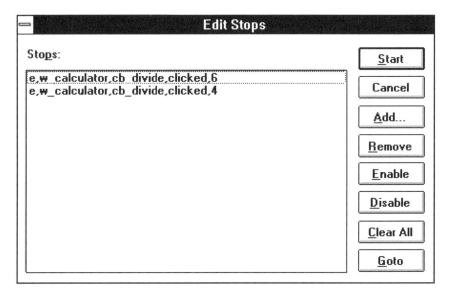

The window labeled Edit Stops lists all the stops in the current application.

The pushbuttons on the Edit Stops window are used as follows:

Start	Starts the application.
Cancel	Closes the Edit Stops window.
Add . . .	Opens the Select Script window to add more stops to the application.
Remove	Removes stops from the debug session.
Enable	Enables a stop that was previously disabled. Must click on the specific stop first to enable.

Disable	Disables a stop that is currently enabled. Must click on the specific stop first to disable.
Clear All	Clears out all the stops in the Stops window.
Goto	Display the script associated with a stop. Must click on a specific stop first.

Executing the Application

Once all breakpoints have been chosen, the developer is ready to start the execution of the application in debug mode. Click on the Start icon from the toolbar to begin the execution.

When a stop is encountered in the script, PowerBuilder suspends execution of the script at that statement *before it has been executed* and the Debug window is displayed again. At this point, the developer may step into the script, continue application execution, display and/or modify variables, or setup a watch list. The Debug window looks like this:

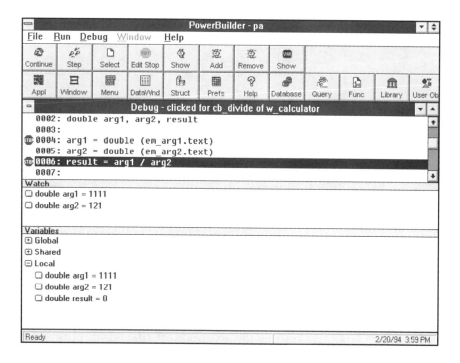

WORKING WITH VARIABLES

To display the application's variables click on the Show Variables icon and the Variables window will display. The Variables window in Debug looks like this:

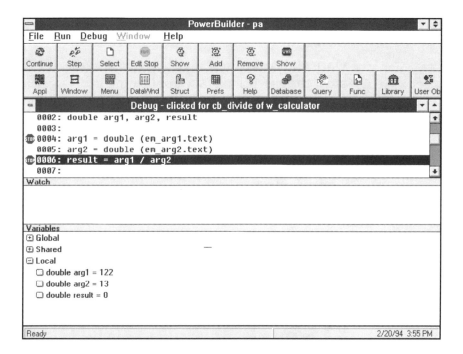

To close the Variables display, click on the Show Variables icon menu selection.

Three variables types (Global, Shared, and Local) will show in the Variables window. A plus sign in the box to the left of the variable type indicates there are variables associated with the variable type. If no variables are associated with the variable type, the box to the left of the label will be blank. Double-clicking on the box in the variable list with the a plus sign will expand the list and display all the variables of that type. A minus sign in the box to the left indicates the list below it can be contracted. When the variables list expands, if there is a plus sign in the box, the developer can double-click to get down to the next level. If the box is blank, the developer may double-click on the variable and the Modify Variable window will appear.

Modifying Application Variables

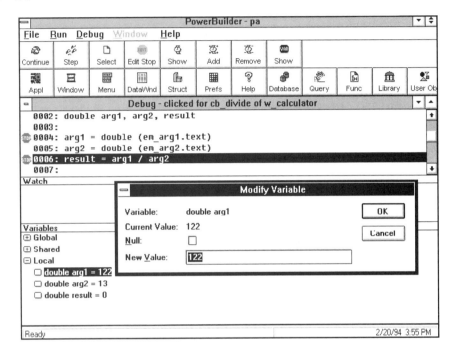

The Modify Variable window shows the variable to modify and its type, the variable's current value, a checkbox indicating if the field is null. The current value of the variable may be changed using the New Value area. Click on the OK pushbutton to return to the Debug window.

WATCH LISTS

A Watch list is used for displaying specific variables and their current values.

To display the Watch window click on the Show icon.

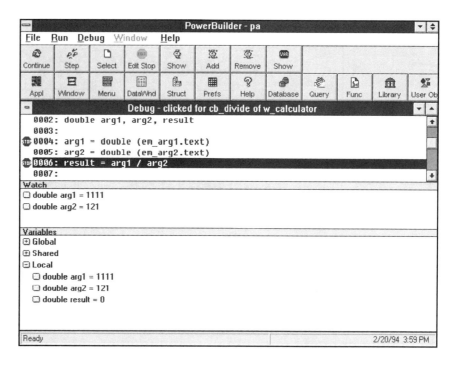

To hide the Watch window click on the Show icon. To add variables to the Watch window, click on the desired variable in the Variable window and click on the Add icon. To remove variables from the Watch window, click on the variable to remove and click on the Remove icon. The developer may step through the script using the Step icon. The developer may click on the Continue icon to execute the script until the next stop.

11

PowerBuilder DataWindows

After completing this chapter, you will be able to build Power-Builder DataWindows. You will learn about the different areas of the DataWindow and the purpose of each one, and you will learn how to use PowerBuilder functions to modify DataWindows. You will also learn how to use PowerScript to access and modify data in DataWindows. In addition, you will discover how to paint SQL to associate with the DataWindow, and we will define computed columns and how to use them.

DATAWINDOW—WHAT IS IT?

The DataWindow object is an intelligent SQL object that manages relational databases without the need to code SQL commands in the application script through the use of specialized PowerBuilder DataWindow functions. The DataWindow allows the developer to present data in eight automatic presentation styles, with data selection from one of four source selection styles. The DataWindow object can retrieve, update, insert, delete, scroll in all directions, print sophisticated reports, and save the data in a number of different file formats. Data can be represented as radiobuttons, check boxes, edit fields, dropdown list boxes, and OLE objects. DataWindows can establish validation criteria and display formats. The DataWindow can also use internal or external code tables for data translation. DataWindows can be changed dynamically at time of execution.

DATAWINDOW AREAS

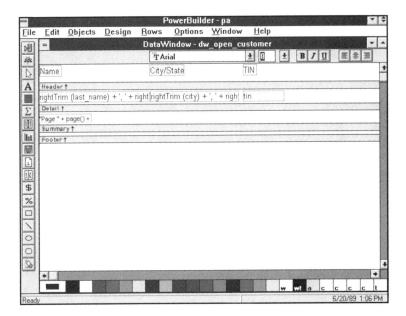

Workspace Area

Area	Purpose
Header	Presents title information and column headings at the top of each page.
Footer	Presents totals and summary information at the bottom of each page.
Detail	Presents data and labels associated with the data. The body repeats as many times as it can within the height of the DataWindow object at execution.
Summary	Presents total and summary information for the entire DataWindow, after the last row displayed in the Detail area. This will appear on the last page of the report only.
Group Header	Presents group heading information.
Group Trailer	Presents totals and summary information for each group. This appears only if you have one or more groups.

DATAWINDOW TOOLBAR

The main functions for creating or modifying a DataWindow are collected on the DataWindow Painter Bar (toolbar).

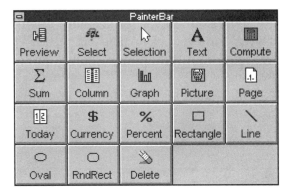

SELECTING A DATAWINDOW

Double-click on the DataWindow Painter icon and the Select DataWindow will open.

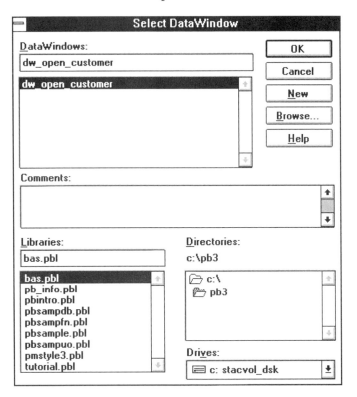

Select the drive and directory of the application .pbl using the Drives and Directories windows.

Select the .pbl that contains the DataWindow(s) from the Libraries window.

To select a DataWindow, click the New pushbutton to create a new DataWindow, click on a specific DataWindow and then click the OK pushbutton, or double-click on the specific Data-Window.

To open a new window, click the New pushbutton.

NEW DATAWINDOWS

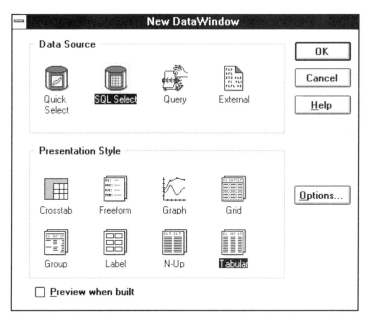

The following elements appear on the New DataWindow screen:

Data Source: Select a method for retrieving the data.

Presentation Style: Select the style for viewing the data.

Preview When Built: When checked, this will cause automatic population of the DataWindow once it is constructed.

Options: Provides generation options for DataWindows. This window appears:

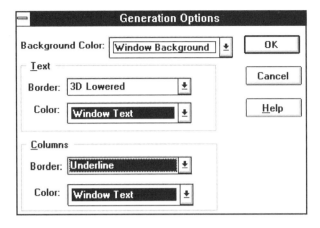

Selecting a Data Source

Quick Select: The QuickSelect options window will appear. Follow the instructions at the top of the window and your data will appear in the Presentation format selected on the NewDataWindow panel.

SQL Select: First the SelectTables window will be offered for you to select the table(s) you wish to use:

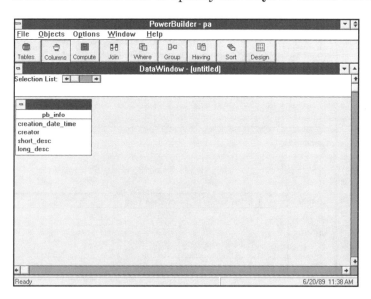

Open: Opens an existing table

New: Opens a new table

Show System Tables: If checked, displays a list of system tables

Once either a new table or an existing table has been selected, the DataWindow appears with the SQL Painter. Use the options from the Painter Bar to specify the SQL to access the data.

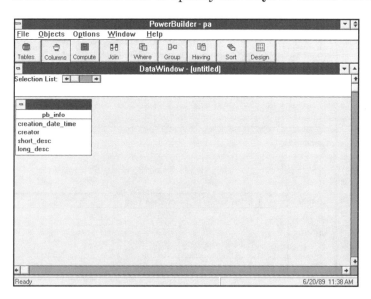

Query: The SelectQuery window will appear for you to select or create a query against the table(s).

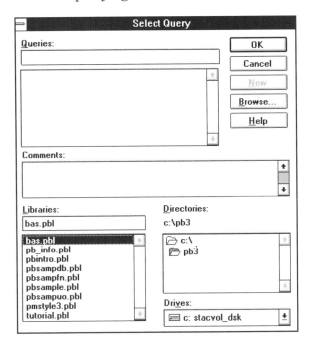

External: The first window opened is the ResultSetDescription for you to specify arguments for a script to populate the Data-Window. Use the Add, Insert, and Delete buttons to modify the result set.

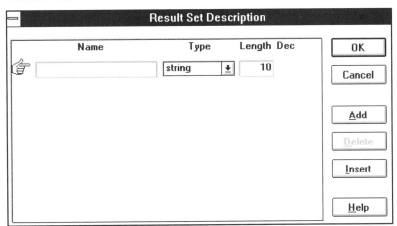

Selecting Presentation Style

Crosstab:

Columns: Select from the pulldown list or type the name of the column(s) to view. You will see one column for each unique value of the database column.

Rows: Select from the pulldown list or type the name of the row(s) to view. You will see one row for each unique value in the database column.

Values: Select a function for the resulting display of the column, such as Sum to summarize the data displayed in the cell.

Freeform:

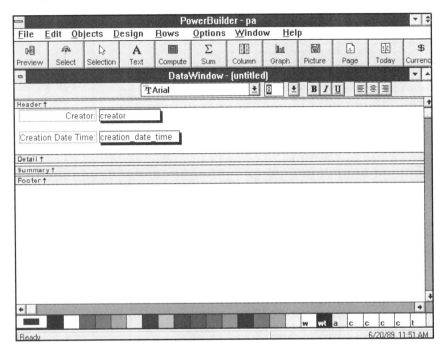

Headers and columns appear in the Detail Area. Header names are generated from information from the Label box in the Extended Definition window in the Database painter.

Graph:

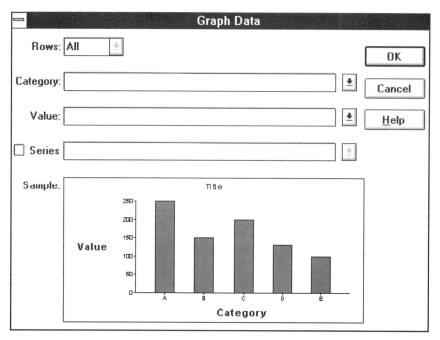

Rows: Select the rows to be graphed from the dropdown list.

Category: Specify the column or expression whose values determine the categories. Select from the dropdown list.

Value: The dropdown list will include the names of all the columns as well as the aggregate functions to count in non-numeric columns and sum numeric columns.

Series: If checked, this will determine grouping by the categories included in the series list.

Grid:

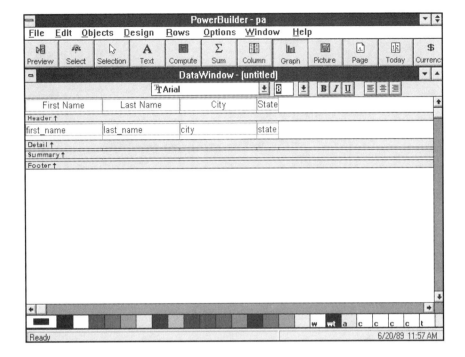

Headers are in the header area; columns are in the detail area. Header names are generated in the Heading box from the Extended Definition in the DataBase painter.

Group: This is a two-step process. First you will be asked to specify Page Header information—the Specify Page Header window will appear first for you to specify Page Header(s).

then you will provide the grouping criteria for the display. After you provide the Page Header details, the Specify Group window appears for you to define the Group Item Expression and provide other details.

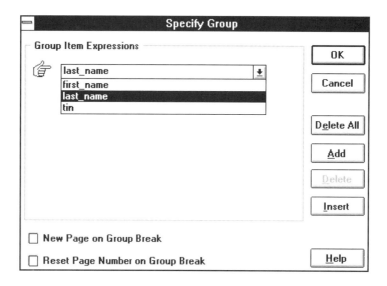

Group Item Expressions: Provides a list of columns which can be used for grouping

New Page on Group Break: If this is checked, will start a new page after a group break

Reset Page Number on Group Break: If this is checked, will start again with page 1 after a group break

Label: This allows you to view your data in the format of printed labels.

N-Up: This style allows you to present two or more rows of data side by side. First you will be asked to provide the number of rows:

After you have chosen the number of rows, you will see the data in a format that is a cross between labels and tabular:

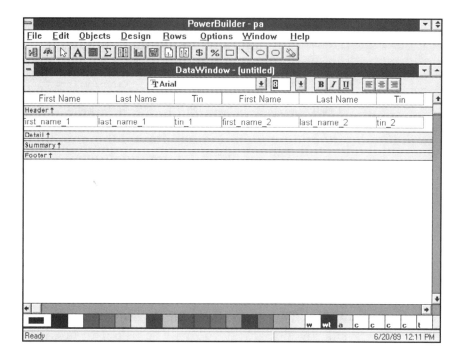

Tabular:

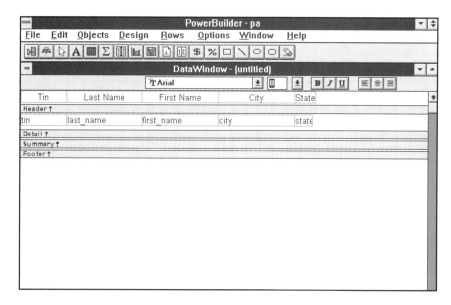

Column headers appear in the Header area. Column names appear in the Detail area. Column headers are defined in the Database painter. If there is no definition, the header name defaults to the column name.

SQL PAINTER BAR

For the Data Source of SQL Select and any Presentation Style, the SQL Painter Bar is your primary source of creating SQL for this DataWindow.

Tables: Displays the list of tables in your application and allows you to choose which table the SQL is for.

Columns: Displays the Columns window for selecting the columns to be included.

Compute: Assists in the creation of a computed column.

Join: Allows joining of tables, but only if at least two tables have been selected in the Select Tables window.

Where ... /Having ... : Assists in defining the where... or having ... criteria for an SQL statement.

Group: Allows setting up group by clauses in the SQL.

Sort: Allows presentation of the data in a specific order.

Design: Returns to the DataWindow painter.

PAINTING SQL

Tables

After the Data Source and Presentation Style have been selected, the developer enters the SQL Painter, unless the source is Script. The developer paints the SQL statement that will be used for the DataWindow by first selecting the table(s) to be used from the Select Tables window:

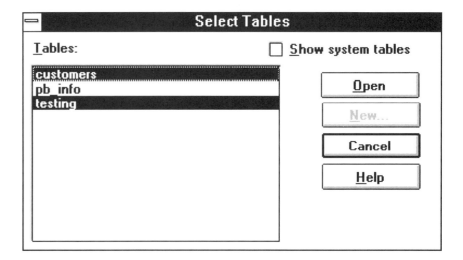

To select the table(s), double-click on the table name, or click on the table name and select the Open pushbutton. When the table selection is complete, click on the Close pushbutton and the Display Columns window will open.

Columns

Display Columns Window

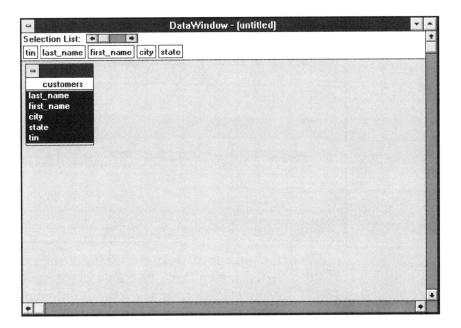

Click on the columns that will be used in the DataWindow. As you are selecting the columns, they will appear on the bar above. Clicking again on a highlighted column will deselect the column. Clicking a column on the selection bar line and dragging that column to a new location in the selection bar modifies the order of display of the columns on the DataWindow. The developer can test the results of the SQL statement generated any time by selecting Preview or Show SQL Syntax options in the Options menu. Preview displays the result set of the SQL select, and Show SQL Syntax displays the syntax of the SQL statement.

When the selection of columns is complete, the developer may either return to the DataWindow painter by selecting Return to DataWindow Painter in the File menu option, or the developer may wish to finetune the SQL statement used in the Data-

Window. The other SQL options are in the Objects menu or on the tool bar.

Other SQL Options:

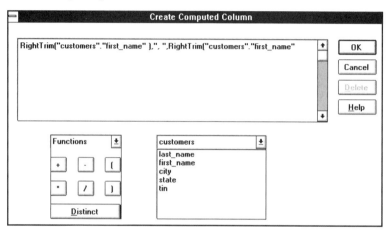

Create Computed Column Build a computed column using a SQL function from the Functions dropdown list box, or use the numeric operators or a combination of the two.

Existing Computed Column *count(first name for....)* is a computed column.

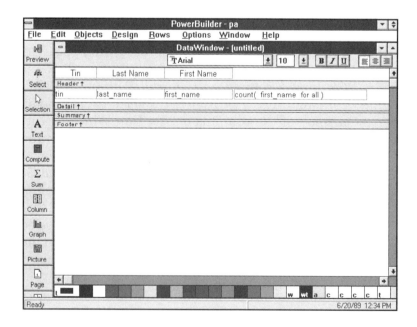

Joins

The Joins option is enabled only if at least two tables have been selected in the Select Tables window.

Click the Joins toolbar selection or menu selection in the Objects menu and the joins cursor will appear. Click on the column in each table that will be joined and a line with an equal sign will appear.

The default is an '=' relationship for the join. To modify, click on the '=' and the Join window will open:

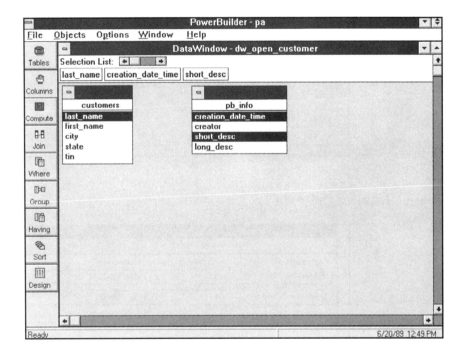

Select the join pushbutton from the Painter Bar

Select column to create outer join from the Select Outer Join Column window if applicable

Select the Delete pushbutton to delete the join

Select the OK pushbutton to exit

When complete, the join will appear on the DataWindow.

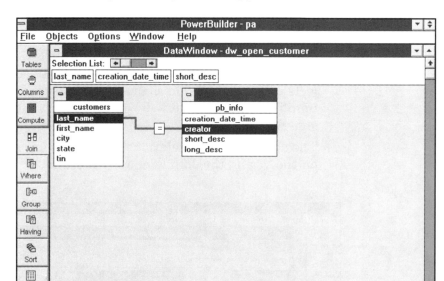

Where/Having Criteria

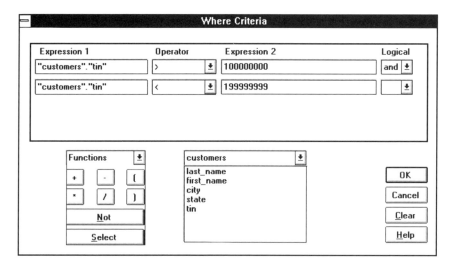

The Where Criteria and the Having Criteria window functionality are exactly the same, therefore the two are combined here. Expression 1 and Expression 2 can be column names, literals, and functions. An operator can be any valid SQL operator (e.g., =, >, <, <>, like, etc.) The example above will create the following Where clause:

```
Select ...
        where customer.c_no = '110'
```

Entering Values Enter expressions and operators in the boxes to indicate the retrieval criteria. To enter the values, click on:

- A table name from the DropDownListBox
- A column name for the selected table in the list box under the table name
- An operator from the DropDownListBox
- A function from the DropDownListBox
- Buttons to insert arithmetic operators and parentheses in the expression
- A NOT button to insert the NOT operator into the expression
- A Select button that opens the Select painter again so that you can paint a nested subquery Select clause
- Logical AND or OR from the DropDownListBox on the field

Click on OK, to return to the Select painter and save the Where criteria. Click on Cancel, to return to the Select painter without saving the Where criteria. Click on Clear, to clear an expression.

Retrieval Arguments The user may need to specify a SQL Select statement that requires that one or more specific values be supplied. To specify retrieval arguments:

1. From the Objects menu, select Retrieval Arguments...

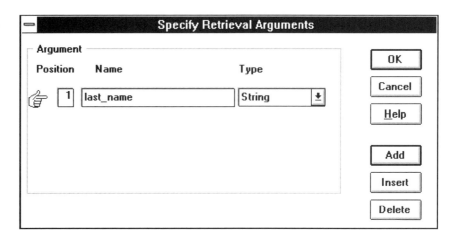

2. For each retrieval argument, specify the name and type, click OK.

Group By Criteria

Grouping Columns

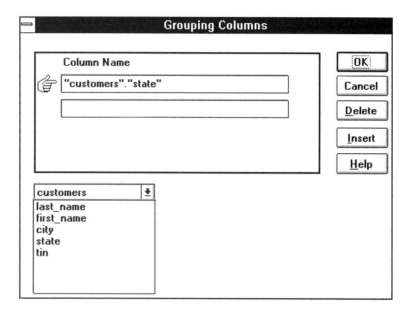

Select the columns to be used in the group by clause of the SQL statement. The example above would create the following Group By clause:

```
Select ...
      group by customer.c_no, customer.state
```

Order By Criteria

Sort Order

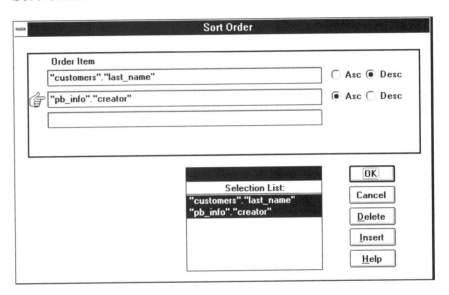

Select columns from the Selection List. Select the appropriate radiobutton to indicate sorting the columns in ascending or descending order. The example above would create the following Order By clause:

```
Select ...
        order by customer.c_no asc, customer.state asc
```

Returning to the DataWindow Painter

At this point the SQL select statement has been created and you are ready to return to the DataWindow painter. Click on the Return to DataWindow Painter selection in the File Menu to return to the DataWindow Painter, or click on the Design (Return) icon on the Painter Bar to return to the DataWindow painter.

The DataWindow painter is where the developer formats the headers and detail fields, defines edit styles of the columns, sets up validation criteria, and performs other operations.

FORMATTING THE DATAWINDOW

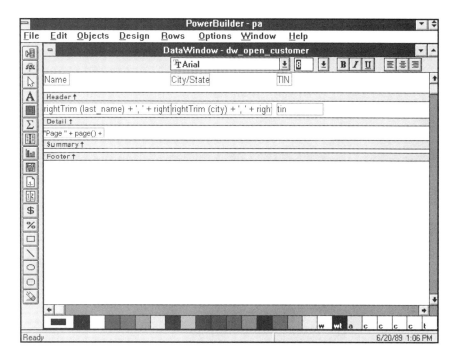

DataWindow Style

> Double-click on whitespace in the DataWindow and the Data-
> Window Style window opens:

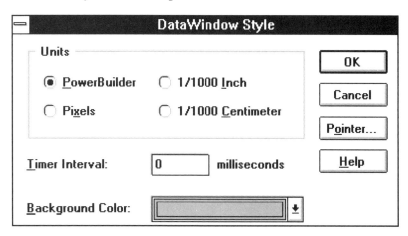

Units: The unit of measure for sizing

Timer Interval: The number of milliseconds until a timer interval event occurs

Background Color: Selected from the Background Color dropdown list box

Pointer: Change the appearance of the pointer by clicking on the pointer button, which brings up the following window:

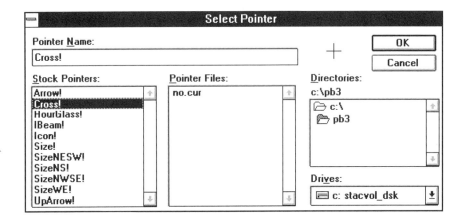

Select the pointer style from one of the stock pointers or use a user-defined pointer file.

Click the OK pushbutton to return to the DataWindow.

Moving Objects

Objects can be rearranged by clicking on the specific field and dragging to new locations. To move multiple objects simultaneously, click on one object then Ctrl/click on the other objects to move. Click and drag the objects to the new locations. Text and column size and style can be modified using the Font and Size dropdown list box on the title toolbar. In the Objects menu and on the toolbar, objects can be used to revise the appearance of the DataWindow. Listed below are objects for this purpose:

The Text menu item or toolbar icon selection adds text to the DataWindow

The Bitmap menu item or toolbar icon selection adds bitmaps to the DataWindow

The Rectangle, Line, Oval, and Round Rectangle menu selections or toolbar icons are used to add geometric objects to the DataWindow

Use the Delete menu item or toolbar icon to delete DataWindow objects. Use the TabOrder menu selection in the Design menu selection to modify the tab order of the DataWindow columns. A tab order of '0' prevents the field from being tabbed to.

Aligning Objects

To align, size, or space DataWindow objects:

Click on the Select menu in the Edit menu selection; then select as suboption: all, above, below, left, right, columns, text, or click on a specific object and press ctrl/click simultaneously to select other objects.

Click on Edit/Align Objects menu selection to align Data-Window objects with the first DataWindow object selected, or

Click on Space Objects menu selection to space DataWindow objects. The spacing between the first two objects selected is the standard, or

Click on Size Objects menu selection to size the DataWindow objects to the size of the first DataWindow object selected.

To change the length of a specific DataWindow object, click on the DataWindow object, move the mouse to the edge of the field, and stretch or contract the object.

DataWindow Header Text

Text Definition Right click on the mouse to bring up the extended attribute list. Select Name and the TextName window will open.

Extended Text Definition

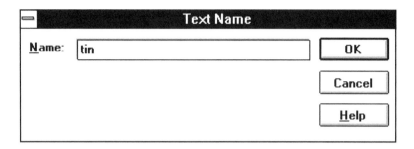

The Text Name box is the name of the text field. Click the OK pushbutton to return to the DataWindow painter.

Display Formats

Column Definition Select the Format dropdown list box in the Edit box to display the applicable formats for the column type, or click the Right mouse button and select Format, or if the field is numeric you can click on either the Percent (%) or Currency ($) Painter Bar button.

Display Formats

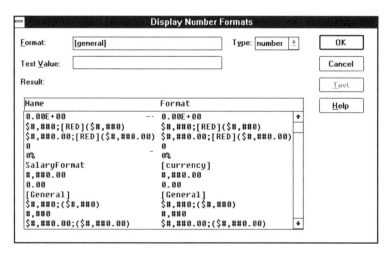

Select a format, which will display in the Format box, enter a number in the Test Value box, then click the Test pushbutton. The formatted result will display on the Result line. Click the OK pushbutton to return to the Column Definition window.

Edit Style

Column Definition Click on the right mouse button, then select Edit Style to modify other attributes of the column:

```
┌─────────────────────────────────────────────────────────────┐
│ ▭                       Edit Style                            │
├─────────────────────────────────────────────────────────────┤
│  N̲ame:  ┌──────────────────────────┬─┐     ┌──────────────┐  │
│         │                          │±│     │      OK      │  │
│         └──────────────────────────┴─┘     └──────────────┘  │
│                                                               │
│  L̲imit:  ┌──────┐       ☒ Auto H̲ Scroll    ┌──────────────┐  │
│          │ 20   │                           │    Cancel    │  │
│          └──────┘       ☐ Auto V̲ Scroll     └──────────────┘  │
│  C̲ase:  ┌────────┬─┐                                          │
│         │ Any    │±│    ☐ H S̲croll Bar      ┌──────────────┐  │
│         └────────┴─┘                        │     Help     │  │
│  A̲ccelerator: ┌───┐     ☐ V Scroll B̲ar      └──────────────┘  │
│               └───┘                                           │
│  ☐ P̲assword            ☐ D̲isplay Only                        │
│                                                               │
│  ☒ A̲uto Selection      ☒ Show F̲ocus Rectangle                │
│                                                               │
│  ☐ R̲equired Field                                            │
│                                                               │
│  ☐ E̲mpty String is NULL                                      │
│                                                               │
│  F̲ormat: ┌──────────────────────────────────┐                │
│          │                                  │                │
│          └──────────────────────────────────┘                │
├─────────────────────────────────────────────────────────────┤
│  ☐ U̲se code table       ☐ Validate using code t̲able          │
│  ┌────────────────────────────────────────┐  ┌────────────┐  │
│  │   Display Value       Data Value       │  │    A̲dd     │  │
│  │                                        │  └────────────┘  │
│  │                                        │  ┌────────────┐  │
│  │                                        │  │   Delete   │  │
│  │                                        │  └────────────┘  │
│  │                                        │  ┌────────────┐  │
│  │                                        │  │   Insert   │  │
│  │                                        │  └────────────┘  │
│  │ Display Count:   0                     │                  │
│  └────────────────────────────────────────┘                  │
└─────────────────────────────────────────────────────────────┘
```

Important Attributes

The **Limit** box specifies the length of the field; a length of '0' means it's unlimited

The **Case** dropdown list box allows the field to be caps, lowercase, or both (any)

There are multiple checkboxes for scroll bars

The developer can assign an accelerator key using the **Accelerator** checkbox

The developer can use **Code Table** options for data translation

Click the OK pushbutton to return to Extended Column Definition window

Select the Edit Style radiobutton to select a style for the column

```
(e.g. Dropdownlistbox, edit box, checkbox, radiobutton)
```

Validation Rules

Column Definition: Specifying Validation Rules Column Validation is opened by clicking on the right mouse button, and selecting Validate from the menu. Column validation is used to specify validation rules for updates performed on a specific column.

Column Validation Definition

```
┌─────────────────────────────────────────────────────────────┐
│ ▬        Column Validation Definition                         │
│ Validation Expression:                                        │
│ ┌───────────────────────────────────┐ ↑  ┌──────────────┐    │
│ │                                   │    │     OK       │    │
│ │                                   │    └──────────────┘    │
│ │                                   │    ┌──────────────┐    │
│ │                                   │    │   Cancel     │    │
│ │                                   │    └──────────────┘    │
│ │                                   │    ┌──────────────┐    │
│ │                                   │    │   Verify     │    │
│ │                                   │ ↓  └──────────────┘    │
│ └───────────────────────────────────┘    ┌──────────────┐    │
│         Functions:          Columns:      │    Help      │    │
│ ┌──┐ ┌──┐ ┌─────────────────┐↑ ┌───────────────┐        │
│ │ +│ │ -│ │isNumber( s )    │  │last_name      │          │
│ └──┘ └──┘ │isSelected()     │  │first_name     │          │
│           │isTime( s )      │  │city           │          │
│ ┌──┐ ┌──┐ │last( #x for all)│  │state          │          │
│ │ x│ │ /│ │left( s, n )     │  │tin            │          │
│ └──┘ └──┘ │leftTrim( s )    │  │               │          │
│           │len( s )         │  │               │          │
│ ┌──┐ ┌──┐ │log( x )         │↓ │               │          │
│ │ (│ │ )│ └─────────────────┘  └───────────────┘          │
│ └──┘ └──┘                                                    │
│ Error Message Expression:                                     │
│ ┌─────────────────────────────────────────────────┐ ↑       │
│ │                                                 │         │
│ │                                                 │ ↓       │
│ └─────────────────────────────────────────────────┘         │
└─────────────────────────────────────────────────────────────┘
```

Validation rules can be specified in the Database painter or the DataWindow painter. If specified in the Database painter, the validation rule will appear in the Validation Expression box on the Column window. Validation rules specified in the Database painter can be changed in the DataWindow painter for the current DataWindow. Changing the validation rule for a DataWindow does not change the rule for the database. Enter an error message in the Error Message Expression box to customize the error message associated with the column validation rule. Click the Verify pushbutton to verify the validation expression.

```
Integer(GetText()) < 1000 and Integer(GetText()) > 100
```

In the example above this validation instruction verifies that column c_no is less than 1000 and greater than 100.

See PowerBuilder Manuals for details on validation rules. Click the OK pushbutton and return to the Column window.

SQL SELECT

Showing the SQL Select

Sometimes after building the DataWindow you realize you forgot a column or you need to pass an argument to the select. The next section discusses modifying the SQL.

Click on the SQL Select button on the Painter Bar to bring up the SQL selection. The options for updating SQL are the same as for defining new SQL. Once changes have been made, the developer may edit the select statement in the display window. Use functions to create aggregate SQL functions from the Painter Bar. To view the SQL, select ShowSQL from the Options menu. Click the OK pushbutton to return to the DataWindow painter.

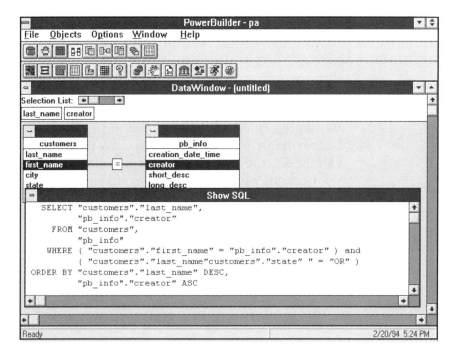

Modifying the SQL Select

Specify Retrieval Arguments Click on the SQL Select button on the Painter Bar, then RetrievalArguments from the Objects menu.

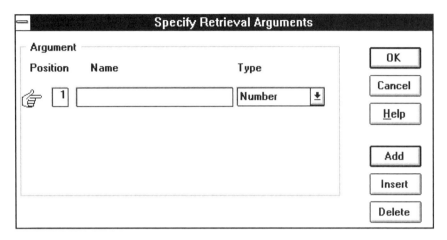

Modify the arguments and click the OK pushbutton to return to the Modify SQL Select window. If you have added a column or a function to the Select, when you return to the DataWindow painter, click on the Column toolbar or menu selection, and then click in the detail portion of the DataWindow. This will add the new column or function to the DataWindow.

FILTERS

Filtering Data

Data retrieved from the database table is limited to the Where clause and retrieve arguments in the Select statement. Retrieve time and runtime space requirements are reduced. Filters are used to limit the data that shows in the DataWindow at runtime. They are expressions that can be True or False. The filter operates at runtime and does not re-execute the SQL statement; it also operates against the data memory.

Defining a Filter

1. From the DataWindow painter, open the Specify Filter window by selecting Filter from the Rows menu.

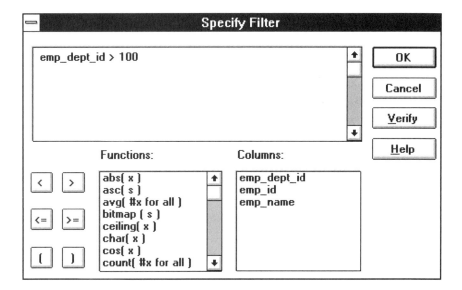

2. Enter text in the filter definition box and insert operators, symbols, functions, and columns.

Argument Specification

After selecting a function, you must specify the required arguments. To create this expression:

```
Month(#1) < 4
```

1. Click on Month. The **d** between the parentheses shows as selected.
2. Click on the column to be filtered. The column name replaces the **d** between the parentheses.

3. With the insertion point at the end of the expression, enter the less than (<) operator and the integer.
4. Click on Verify, then click on OK.

A filter defined in the DataWindow painter applies to the Data-Window until deleted. A filter can be changed at runtime.

Temporary Filter

From the test window only, you can work with a temporary filter. This filter will be deleted when you leave the test window.

SORTING THE DATAWINDOW ROWS

Click on the Sort... selection in the Rows menu selection and the Specify Sort Columns window will open:

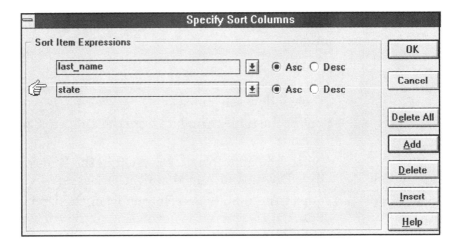

Select the columns to sort on and select asc (ascending) or desc (descending) sort order. Selecting the column again deselects that column from the sort window. Click Clear All to erase all the columns that are in the sort window. Click the OK pushbutton to return to the DataWindow painter.

UPDATE CRITERIA

Click the Update selection in the Rows menu selection and the Specify Update. The Characteristics window will open:

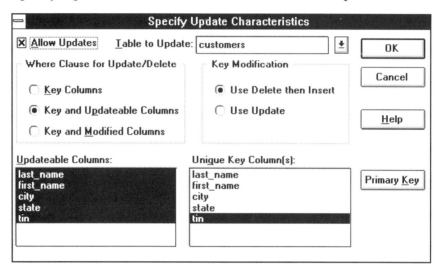

First click the checkbox Allow Updates to enable the rest of the window selections.

Select the table to update from the Table to Update dropdown list box.

Select the appropriate selection in the Where Clause for Update/Delete and Key Modification boxes.

Select the updatable columns from the Updatable Columns box. This is where the developer can restrict specific columns from being updated.

Select the columns that will insure a unique key from the Unique Key Box.

Click the Default Primary Key pushbutton if you want the unique columns to be the primary key created in the Data-Base painter.

Click the OK pushbutton to return to the DataWindow painter.

SAVING THE DATAWINDOW

1. From the File Menu, Click on Save or Save As…

2. Specify name and library and click on OK

THE DATAWINDOW CONTROL

The DataWindow object is a special PowerBuilder object that allows the user to display and manipulate SQL database information without coding SQL in the script. To use a DataWindow in your application, first you create it in the DataWindow painter, then you place a DataWindow control on an application window in the Window painter, and finally you associate a DataWindow object with the control in the Window painter or associate it with script at runtime. At runtime Powerbuilder creates an instance of the DataWindow.

The DataWindow Control has a *style* that is determined by the *attributes* and *events* which can trigger the execution of *scripts*. PowerBuilder has a group of *functions* specifically for the DataWindow control.

DataWindow Control Attributes

DataWindow Attributes

Attribute	Datatype	Description
Backcolor	Long	Long Integer indicating background color
Border	Boolean	Adds border around DataWindow object
ControlMenu	Boolean	Adds a control menu
DataObject	String	Name of the DataWindow object
DragAuto	Boolean	Indicates whether PowerBuilder will put the control automatically in drag mode
DragIcon	String	Name of the icon used when the user drags the control
Enabled	Boolean	Indicates whether the object can send or receive messages
Height	Integer	Height of the object in PowerBuilder units
HscrollBar	Boolean	Indicates whether to display a horizontal scroll bar
Icon	String	Name of the icon when a DataWindow is minimized
Maxbox	Boolean	Indicates if a maximize box is on the DataWindow
MinBox	Boolean	Indicates if a minimize box is on the DataWindow
Resizable	Boolean	Allows the user to resize the DataWindow
Taborder	Unsigned Integer	A number indicating the tabbing sequence of the DataWindow control
Tag	String	String that contains the tag value
Title	String	String containing the Title of the DataWindow
TitleBar	Boolean	Indicates if a title bar is present—a title bar is needed to move the control
Visible	Boolean	Indicates whether the control is visible or invisible
VscrollBar	Boolean	Indicates whether a vertical scroll bar is used
Width	Integer	Width of the DataWindow in PowerBuilder units
X	Integer	Distance from the left edge the control will be in PowerBuilder units
Y	Integer	Distance from the top the control will be in PowerBuilder units

Examples of Script Using DataWindow Attributes

Disabling the DataWindow control

```
dw_1.enabled = FALSE
```

Making the DataWindow control invisible

```
dw_1.visible = FALSE
```

Associating the DataWindow control with a DataWindow object

```
dw_1.DataObject = "dw_2"
```

DataWindow Events

DataWindow Events

Event	Occurs When . . .
Clicked	User clicks on the DataWindow
DBError	Database Error occurs
Double-clicked	User double-clicks on the DataWindow
DragDrop	Dragged object is dropped on target object
DragEnter	Dragged object enters target object
DragLeave	Dragged object leaves target object
DragWithin	Dragged object is within target object
EditChanged	The user types in an edit control
GetFocus	An object receives focus
ItemChanged	A field in the DataWindow is modified and it loses focus
ItemError	A field is modified, it loses focus, but fails the validation test
ItemFocusChanged	The current item changes in a DataWindow
LoseFocus	DataWindow object loses focus
Other	Event other than a PowerBuilder event
PrintEnd	Printing of a DataWindow ends
PrintPage	Before each page is formatted for printing
PrintStart	Contents of a DataWindow begins printing
Resize	DataWindow is resized
RetrieveEnd	Retrieval for a DataWindow is complete
RetrieveRow	After the retrieval of a row
RetrieveStart	Retrieval of a DataWindow is about to begin
RowFocusChanged	Current row changes in a DataWindow
ScrollHorizontal	The user scrolls right or left
ScrollVertical	The user scrolls up or down
SQLPreview	After a Retrieve, Update, or ReselectRow function call and immediately before it is executed
UpdateEnd	All the updates from the DataWindow to the database are complete
UpdateStart	After the DataWindow receives the update message but before the update starts

See PowerBuilder manuals or Help facility for more detail on PowerBuilder events.

DataWindow Functions

Control-Related Functions The DataWindow control-related functions are numerous and would take several pages just to list. The following tables show some of the more commonly used functions. For further information see the PowerBuilder manuals or Help facility.

Manipulation Functions

Function	Description
DeleteRow	Delete current row
GetClickedColumn	Get number of current column
GetClickedRow	Get number of current row
GetColumn	Get specific column
GetItemDate	Get Date from specific row and column
GetItemDateTime	Get DateTime from specific row and column
GetItemNumber	Get Number from specific row and column
GetItemString	Get String from specific row and column
GetItemTime	Get Time from specific row and column
GetRow	Get a specific row
GetSelectedRow	Get current row
SetItem	Set a specific row and column to a value
InsertRow	Insert a new row
Reset	Clear values in DataWindow
Retrieve	Retrieve data into DataWindow
SaveAs	Save contents of the DataWindow in a specific format
ScrollNextPage	Scroll next page
ScrollNextRow	Scroll next row
ScrollPriorPage	Scroll prior page
ScrollPriorRow	Scroll prior row
Update	Update changes made in the DataWindow to the database

Informational Functions

Function	Description
DeletedCount	Count of number of deleted rows in the delete buffer
ModifiedCount	Count of the number of modified rows in the modified buffer
RowCount	Number of rows available to the DataWindow
SetTransObject	Connects DataWindow to a Transaction object

USING DATAWINDOWS

Coding Examples

1. Retrieving data into a DataWindow without arguments. The SetTransObject is required before the Retrieve can execute:

```
SetTransObject(dw_1,SQLCA)
 Retrieve(dw_1)
```

2. Retrieving data into a DataWindow with two arguments. The SetTransObject is required before the Retrieve can execute:

```
SetTransObject(dw_1,SQLCA)
 Retrieve(dw_1, str_arg1,str_arg2)
```

3. Determining how many rows are available to the Data-Window:

```
Integer row_count
 row_count = RowCount(dw_1)
```

4. Determining how many rows have been modified in the Data-Window:

```
Integer modified_count
 modified_count = ModifiedCount(dw_1)
```

5. Selecting a specific column in a DataWindow, the following code could be used in the clicked or double-clicked event:

```
If GetClickedRow(dw_1) > 0 then
      SelectRow(dw_1, 0, FALSE)
      SelectRow( dw_1,GetClickedRow(dw_1), TRUE)
      str_col1 =
GetItemString(dw_1,GetClickedRow(dw_1),1)
else
      beep(2)
end if
```

a. The If GetClickedRow... checks to see if a valid row was clicked on. If it is valid, the function returns a number greater then zero. If the number equals zero, the user clicked on a header or footer and the terminal will beep.

b. SelectRow(dw_1, 0, FALSE)—Deselects (unhighlights) all rows in the DataWindow.

c. SelectRow(dw_1,GetClickedRow(dw_1), TRUE)—Selects or highlights the row that was clicked on.

d. str_col1 = GetItemString(dw_1,GetClickedRow(dw_1),1)— Gets the string that is in column 1 and the row that was selected, and puts it in the variable str_col1.

6. Retrieving data into a DataWindow then printing the Data-Window:

```
SetTransObject(dw_1,SQLCA)
 Retrieve(dw_1)
print(dw_1,TRUE)
```

a. SetTransObject(dw_1,SQLCA)—Connects the DataWindow to the Transaction object SQLCA

b. Retrieve(dw_1)—Retrieve data into the DataWindow

c. print(dw_1,TRUE)—Print the DataWindow

12

DataWindow Reporting

After completing this chapter, you will be able to create reports using the PowerBuilder DataWindow. You will also learn how to use PowerBuilder functions and options to tailor DataWindow reports. We will discuss how to change the background color and text attributes, and you will learn how to define edit styles, and enhance the design of the report.

PowerBuilder has a group of functions used for tailoring the DataWindow. These functions are added by using the Computed Column toolbar icon. You will learn how to design Computed Columns.

To enhance the appearance of your DataWindow you will want to place pictures in it. We will discuss the way these pictures are placed and how to save them.

FEATURES

The PowerBuilder DataWindow allows flexibility in report design

PowerBuilder supplies a multitude of functions useful in designing reports

The PowerBuilder DataWindow can create reports easily and quickly

COLOR AND RIBBON

To Select Background Color

You can set the background and text colors for data, text, and drawing objects from the DataWindow painter by clicking Color with the right mouse button.

To Select Font and Size

From the ribbon on the DataWindow painter you can edit the text and select type font, size, style, and justification.

1. Select the text.
2. Click on the FontDropDownListBox; choose one of the fonts or enter the name of the font.
3. Click on the SizeDropDownListBox; choose one of the sizes or enter the size number of choice.

To Select Type Style and Justification

1. Select the text.
2. Click on: Bold, Italic, and/or Underline; Left, Right, or Center.

DESIGN ENHANCEMENT

To Change Column Headings

1. From the column's popup menu, select Header.
2. In the Heading box, type in the new text. To define multiline headings, separate lines of text with special codes that represent Carriage Return/Line Feed, ~r~n.

EXAMPLE: Type in Name~r~nTitle it will display as:

Name

Title

To Insert Text

1. Click the Text icon.
2. Place cursor in the selected DataWindow.
3. Type the text.
4. Select font, size, and style for the text. Select foreground and background colors.

To Change Font, Style, Size, or Color

To change font, style, or color, select the text or columns.

To change type style, click the Style buttons: Bold, Italic, or Underline.

To change type size, choose a size from the DropDownListBox or enter a size.

To change font, choose a font from the font DropDownListBox or enter a font name.

To change color, from the Color item on the popup menu choose a background and/or text colors.

To Insert a Drawing Object

1. Select the drawing object.
2. In the DataWindow, click where you want the object to display.
3. Make any adjustments you want to the object, resize it, move it.
4. Using the drawing object's popup menu, you can change foreground and background colors, line style, and patterns.

Additional Column Definition

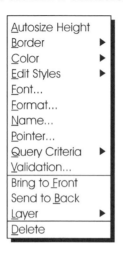

To specify a border, an edit style, a display format, and input validation for a column, click the right mouse button on the column name. To set the suitable menu item, click on that menu item.

To Define an Edit Style

Edit style can be defined for checkboxes and radiobuttons, Single-LineEdits and DropDownListBoxes.

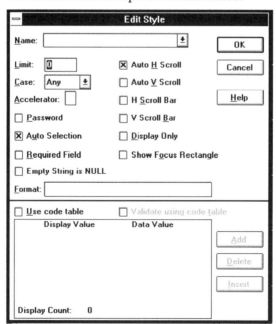

1. From the popup menu, click Edit Styles then Edit from the cascading menu.

   From the **Limit** box you can restrict the number of characters the user can enter.

   From the **Case** box you can convert the case of characters.

   From the **Password** box you can have entered values display as asterisks for sensitive data.

   From the **Display Only** box you can allow users to tab to the column but not change the value.

   From the **Use Code Table** you can determine which values are displayed to users and which are stored in the database.

2. To return to the DataWindow Painter click OK.

CREATING THE DATAWINDOW REPORT

Creating the DataWindow for reporting is the same as previously explained in chapter 11. Once the basic DataWindow has been created, you can add reporting functionality to the DataWindow to tailor the reports to specific needs.

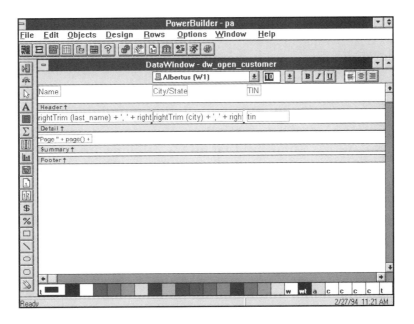

A quick review of the basic DataWindow we used in chapter 11 follows.

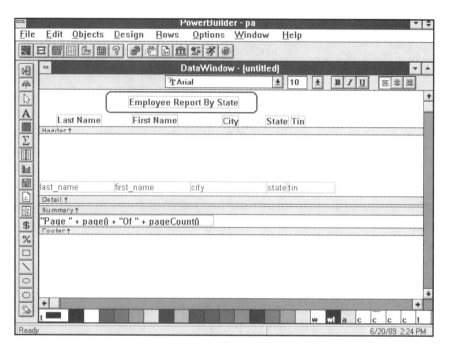

1. The first thing to add would be the report headers.
    Move all the columns and column heading down on the report to make room for the heading.
    a. Click and drag the Detail Bar and the Header Bar down to make room at the top for the Title
    b. Click on the first column and ctrl/click the rest of the columns so that all the columns are selected
    c. Click and drag the columns down to make room
    d. Do the same with the headers
    Select the Text toolbar icon or menu option and place the text on the DataWindow. Change the font and size accordingly by selecting the font style and size. Double-click on the report header and select a border option (e.g., box, shadow box, underline).

2. Change the column headings to meaningful names. Click on the column heading and modify the text on the toolbar. (Note: This could have been done in the Extended Column Definition in the Database painter)

3. Add a border to the column by double-clicking on the column headings and picking a border option. For example purposes we will use Underline.

4. Move objects by clicking on the objects and dragging them to new locations. To move multiple objects simultaneously click on the first object then ctrl/click on the others; click and drag on one object and all the rest will follow the mouse. To reset the multiple selection, click on anything not selected.

5. Don't forget the Align Objects, Space Objects, and Size Objects options in the Edit menu selection.

Column Formatting

Columns can be modified by clicking the right mouse button on the column to open the Change menu. Select the option to be changed, or highlight the column to be changed from the list of columns by selecting ColumnSpecifications from the Rows menu. Common reporting options are changing the Display Format and/or Adding/Changing the Border option.

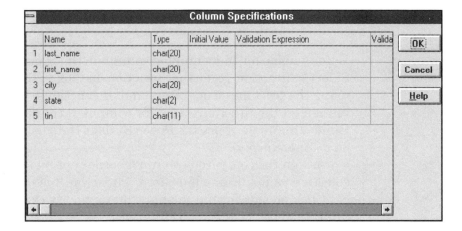

Computed Columns

PowerBuilder has a group of functions used for tailoring the Data-Window. These functions are added to the DataWindow by clicking on the Computed Column toolbar icon or menu option, then clicking on the area in the DataWindow where you wish to add the computed column. The Computed Field Definition window will open.

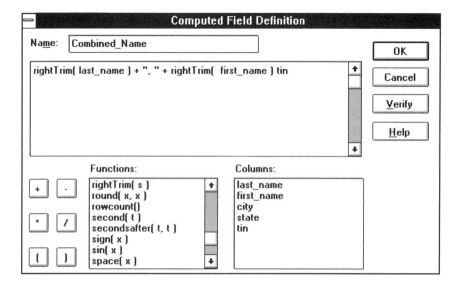

Enter a name for the computed column in the Name box if needed. Select a function from the Function listbox or build your own using the arithmetic operators and/or functions. For more information on the functions used for computed columns, see Power-Builder manuals or use the PowerBuilder Help facility and search on *computed columns*.

Assign the computed column a border option from the Border selection radiobuttons if desired. The default is none.

Click on the Format pushbutton to modify the computed column format.

Setting Tab Order

A default tab value is initiated in the DataWindow painter. The TAB key is used to move from one DataWindow object to another in the order in which they were placed in the workspace.

To Change Tab Sequence

1. From the Design Menu, select Tab Order.

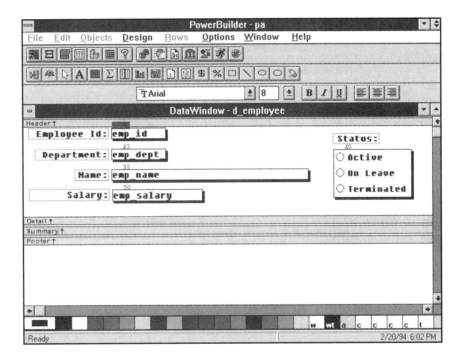

2. With the mouse or the TAB key, select the tab value you want changed.
3. Setting the tab value to zero will prevent the pointer from stopping at a column when the user presses TAB or Shift+TAB.
4. To save changes and close the Tab Order window, select Tab Order from the Design menu again.

Adding and Restoring Columns

In the DataWindow, you can add columns and restore columns that you deleted.

To Add A Column

1. From the toolbar or Edit Data Source from the Design menu, click the SQL Select button. The Select painter redisplays.
2. Click the column to add it to the list.

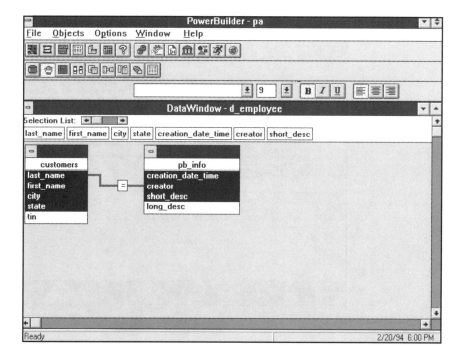

3. From the toolbar, click the Design button. The DataWindow painter displays.
4. From the Objects menu, click the Column button.
5. Click at the point where you want to insert the column.

Adding Pictures

To enhance the appearance of your DataWindow, you can place pictures in it. These pictures must be a .bmp file column in a DataWindow. The bitmap can be database columns, static (file names), or computed columns defined using the bitmap function.

To Display a Bitmap

1. Using the right mouse button, click on the column name
2. From the pop-up menu, select Edit Styles

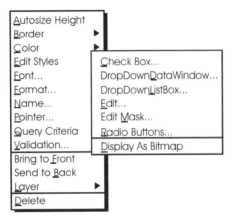

3. From the cascading menu, select Display As Bitmap
When placing the bitmap as a static object in a DataWindow, the name of the bitmap file is not stored in the database.

TESTING A DATAWINDOW REPORT

Test the DataWindow by selecting the Preview option in the Design Menu.

Click the Close pushbutton to return to DataWindow Painter.

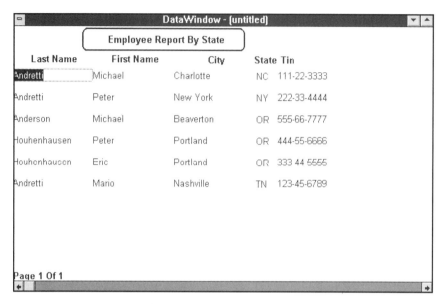

ADDING FINAL DETAILS

Group Header and Trailer Areas

You can create headers and trailers for each group.

You can place a table column or a computed field in the header or trailer area of a group.

To Place a Column in the Header or Trailer Area of a Group

1. Select the column you want deleted.
2. Drag the column into the group header or trailer where you want it positioned.

To Place a Computed Field in the Header or Trailer Area of a Group

1. From the toolbar, click Computed Field.
2. Click at the point in the group header or trailer where the computed field should go. The Computed Field Definition window is presented.
3. Enter a name for the computed field. This name can be used later for referencing this field.
4. Click on the name of the field you want displayed in the header or trailer.
5. Click OK.

Page Numbers

Using the menu item 'Page n of n' or the toolbar button, you can add page numbers to your reports.

1. From the Object menu, click the Page icon or select Page n of n Computed Field.
2. At the location where you want the page number to appear, usually in the trailer area, click. A computed field is placed at that point.

```
EXAMPLE:  Page n or nnn
n = page number - nnn = total number of pages
```

The functions to create Page n of nnn:

- Page()
- PageCount()

These functions can be used in computed fields in a DataWindow.

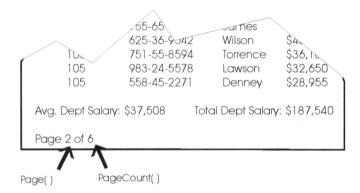

Page( )   PageCount( )

Suppressing Repeating Values

You might want to suppress the display of a repeating value for a column, such as in a column of Department IDs. When suppressing a repeating value, at the start of each new page the value displays. If you are using groups, the value displays each time in a higher group.

Employee Salaries

Department Name: Sales

Department ID	Employee SSN	Last Name	Salary
105	155-65-9875	James	$43,500
	625-36-9542	Wilson	$46,250
	751-55-8594	Torrence	$36,185
	983-24-5578	Lawson	$32,650
	558-45-2271	Denney	$28,955

Avg. Dept Salary: $37,508   Total Dept Salary: $187,540

Page 2 of 6

From the Rows menu on the DataWindow Painter, select Suppress Repeating Values.

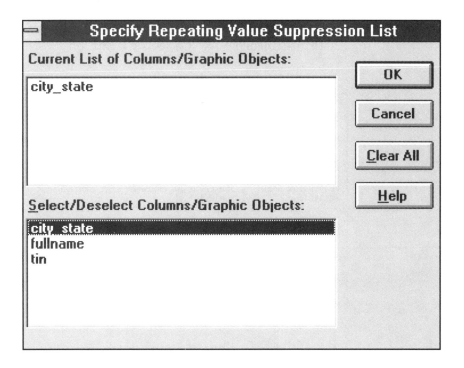

PRINTING REPORTS

PowerScript supplies several functions that you can use to print lists and reports.

DataWindow Print Function

This function tells the DataWindow to send its contents to the current printer specified in Print Setup.

To format: <dw_control_name>.Print()

Example: `dw_employee_contact.Print()`

Managing Print Jobs

The basic print functions are:

Print()	Sends strings to the current printer
PrintOpen()	Starts a print job
PrintClose()	Stops a print job
PrintSetup()	Calls the Printer Setup dialog box
PrintCancel()	Cancels a print job

```
INT JOB_Print
Job_Print =        PrintOpen()
PrintBitMap        ( Job_Print,"F:\WINDOWS\BITMAPS\CURRENCY.BMP",5,10,0,0 )
PrintClose         ( Job_Print )
Job_Print =        PrintOpen()
PrintDataWindow    ( Job_Print,dw_employee_list_permanent )
PrintDataWindow    ( Job_Print,dw_employee_list_temporary )
PrintDataWindow    ( Job_Print,dw_employee_list_contract )
PrintClose         ( Job_Print )
```

DATAWINDOW GROUPING

From the DataWindow painter, the Create Group creates a trailer area in the DataWindow for that group. This allows the report to do subtotals by the named group. From the Rows menu select Create Group. The Specify Group window is presented.

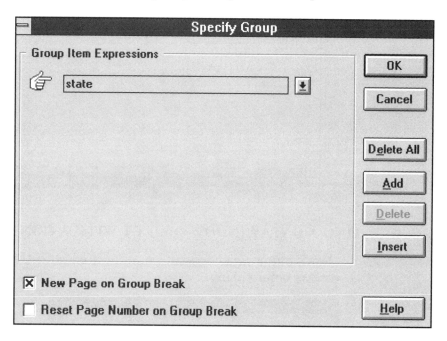

In the example above, a group is created with the column state, and the new page checkbox is checked. When testing the Data-Window, this will generate a page break when the value of state changes.

Clicking on the Computed Column icon or menu selection and then clicking in the Trailer area we can add the sum (balance for group 1) function to create subtotals. Click on the Text toolbar icon or menu option to add text for the Grand Total label and the Page label. Click on the DataWindow to add the text.

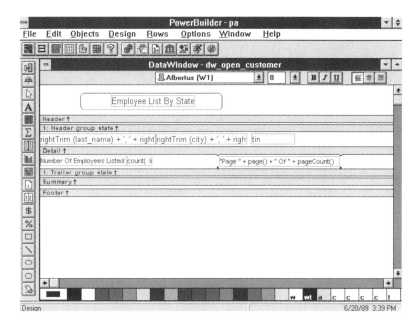

ASSOCIATING A DATAWINDOW OBJECT WITH A CONTROL

DataWindow objects must be associated with the DataWindow control before using.

1. With the right mouse button on the DataWindow control in the Window painter, click on the Select DataWindow window. Select Change DataWindow.
2. Select the DataWindow object to be used on this window.

Your scripts will reference the DataWindow control that you created in the Window painter. Data acquired through the SQL Select statement connected with the DataWindow object displays through this control.

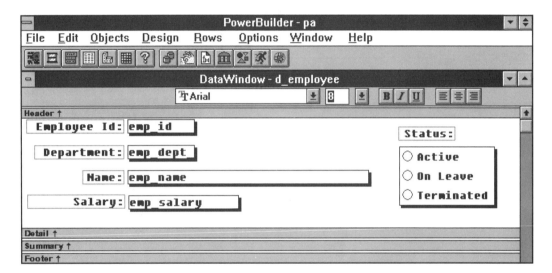

The Edit Control

The user sees the presentation of the DataWindow and types in the edit control. Data moves between the memory structure and the edit control.

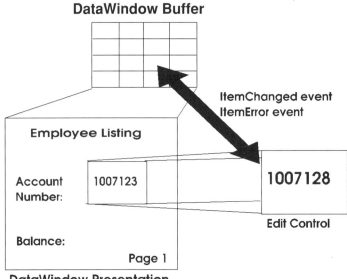

DataWindow Buffer

ItemChanged event
ItemError event

Employee Listing

Account
Number: 1007123   **1007128**

                                              Edit Control

Balance:

                        Page 1

DataWindow Presentation

ADDING THE REPORT TO THE APPLICATION

After the report design has been completed, place the DataWindow control onto the appropriate application window and associate the DataWindow object with the DataWindow control. The developer may use PowerBuilder script to modify, access, and print the report. A common technique is hiding the DataWindow control, adding a print pushbutton or menu selection to retrieve data into the DataWindow, and then printing the report.

Coding Example:

```
SetTransObject((dw_1, SQLCA)
 Retrieve(dw_1,Arg1,Arg2,...)
 Print(dw_1,TRUE)
```

SetTransObject sets up the DataWindow with the transaction object SQLCA.

Retrieve populates the DataWindow. Arg1, Arg2 are optional arguments, they are only needed if the DataWindow is an SQL Select with Arguments.

Print is used to print the DataWindow. The second parameter specifies if a print messagebox window will appear. See Power-Builder manuals or help screens for more detail on print functions.

ACCESSING A DATABASE

You must initiate a Transaction Object before you can access the database through a DataWindow. A Transaction Object, a non-graphic object, communicates information about your database to PowerBuilder. PowerBuilder stores database information in the transaction object. A function communicates that information to the DataWindow and determines how it handles database processing.

Transaction Object

A default transaction object named SQLCA is created in Power-Builder when you start to execute an application. There are fifteen fields in a transaction object: Ten fields are used to identify and connect to the database; five fields return status information from the database management system.

Note: There can be more than one connection to a database.

The following chart shows transaction object fields you use when you connect to a database.

Transaction Object Fields to Connect to a Database

Field Name	Database	Value
AutoCommit	All	True/False
Database	All	Name of specific database
DBMS	All	String containing the name of your DBMS (Sybase, Gupta, Oracle...)
DBParm	WATCOM/SQL™	Information specific to the database
DBPass	Allbase™	Password for connecting to the database
	Gupta SQLBase®	
Lock	Allbase	Isolation level
	Gupta SQLBase	
LogID	Database Gateway™	Name of the user who will log on to the database server
	ORACLE® Server	
	Sybase/SQL Server™	
LogPass	Database Gateway	Password to log on to the server
	ORACLE Server	
	Sybase/SQL Server	
ServerName	Database Gateway	Name of the database server
	ORACLE Server	
	Sybase/SQL Server	
UserID	Allbase	Name of the user who will connect
	Gupta SQLBase	

This next chart shows Transaction Object Fields used to return information from the database management system after each request is completed:

Transaction Object Fields to Return Information

Field Name	Database	Return Value
SQLCode	All	Success or failure code for the most-recent SQL operation: 0 OK 100 Not Found −1 SQL Error
SQLNRows	All	Number of rows affected
SQLDBCode	All	Database vendor-specific error code
SQLErrText	All	Database vendor-specific error message
SQLReturnData	ODBC, Informix	Additional information, DBMS vendor-specific

User-Defined Transaction Object When you are using more than one database at a time in an application, you can create other transaction objects. To create a transaction object in a script:

1. Declare the transaction object, TR1:

   Transaction TR1

2. Create the transaction object:

   TR1 = create transaction

Note: The range of the transaction object variable determines how long you can access it. If declared in a script, it will go out of range when the script ends.

Assign Values to Transaction Object Fields Values must be assigned to transaction object fields used to connect to the database before using any transaction object, even the default transaction object.

FORMAT: `<transaction-name>.<field-name>=<value>`

EXAMPLE:

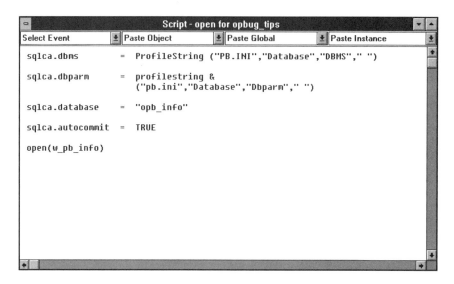

Destroying the Transaction Object When your script completes its need for a transaction object, you should destroy it to disengage the resources it is holding.

FORMAT: `Destroy<transaction-name>`

EXAMPLE: `Destroy TR1`

TRANSACTION MANAGEMENT

SetTransObject

The SetTransObject function initiates the values for a Data-Window transaction object. The current values of the database identification fields in the specified transaction object are retained by the DataWindow when you execute a SetTransObject function. When the DataWindow prepares and executes SQL statements, these values are used. The SetTransObject function gives you more control over the transaction (i.e., connection duration, row locking, transaction commit, and/or rollback). When using the SetTransObject function, the script issues the Connect, Commit, Rollback, and Disconnect statements.

Connect: Establishes the connection and starts the transaction

Disconnect: Removes the connection and ends the transaction

Commit: Applies changes to the database

Rollback: Rolls data changes back to the last Commit or Connect

FORMAT: `<dw_control_name>.SetTransObject(<transaction>)`

EXAMPLE:

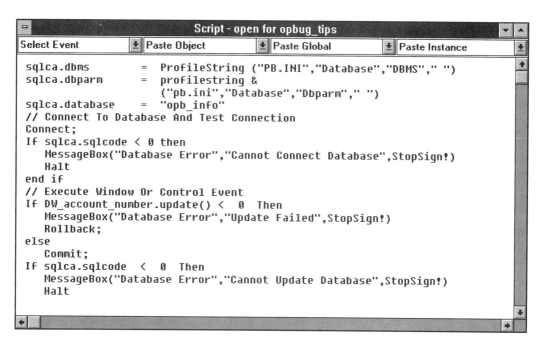

```
┌──────────────────────────────────────────────────────────────────┐
│ ⊖                    Script - open for opbug_tips          ▼  ▲    │
├──────────────────────────────────────────────────────────────────┤
│ Select Event       ± Paste Object  ± Paste Global  ± Paste Instance ±│
├──────────────────────────────────────────────────────────────────┤
sqlca.dbms        =   ProfileString ("PB.INI","Database","DBMS"," ")
sqlca.dbparm      =   profilestring &
                      ("pb.ini","Database","Dbparm"," ")
sqlca.database    =   "opb_info"
// Connect To Database And Test Connection
Connect;
If sqlca.sqlcode < 0 then
   MessageBox("Database Error","Cannot Connect Database",StopSign!)
   Halt
end if
// Execute Window Or Control Event
If DW_account_number.update() < 0  Then
   MessageBox("Database Error","Update Failed",StopSign!)
   Rollback;
else
   Commit;
If sqlca.sqlcode  < 0  Then
   MessageBox("Database Error","Cannot Update Database",StopSign!)
   Halt
```

DATAWINDOW FUNCTIONS

There are many PowerScript functions that you can use to request that the DataWindow perform specific activities. The most commonly used functions are listed in the following chart:

Most Commonly Used DataWindow Functions

Name	Format	Description
Clear	<dw_control_name>.Clear()	Clears the selected text in the current field of the DataWindow object
Copy	<dw_control_name>.Copy()	Copies the selected text in the current field of the DataWindow to the clipboard
Cut	<dw_control_name>.Cut()	Cuts the selected text from the current field of the DataWindow and stores it in the clipboard
DeleteRow	<dw_control_name>.DeleteRow(<row>)	Removes the specified row from the specified DataWindow
GetClickedrow	<dw_control_name>.GetClickedRow()	Returns the number of the row in the DataWindow that the user clicked or double-clicked
GetItemx	<dw_control_name>.GetItemDate(<row>,<column>)	Returns the data (in the same data type) from the DataWindow row and column specified
	<dw_control_name>.GetItemDateTime((<row>,<column>))	
	<dw_control_name>.GetItemNumber(<row>,<column>)	
	<dw_control_name>.GetItemString(<row>,<column>)	
	<dw_control_name>.GetItemTime(<row>,<column>)	
GetRow	<dw_control_name>.GetRow()	Returns a long containing the current row number in the specified DataWindow
GetText	<dw_control_name>.GetText()	Returns the text that is current in the edit box
InsertRow	<dw_control_name>.InsertRow(<row>)	Inserts a new row before the specified row in the DataWindow
Reset	<dw_control_name>.Reset()	Completely clears all rows of the DataWindow

Name	Format	Description
Retrieve	<dw_control_name>.Retrieve()	Causes the specified DataWindow to retrieve rows from the database
Retrieve with retrieve arguments	<dw_control_name>.Retrieve(<arg1>,<arg2>,...)	Use the Retrieve function with substitution arguments to provide specific values to the SELECT statement for the DataWindow
RowCount	<dw_control_name>.RowCount()	Returns the number of rows currently available in the DataWindow
SaveAs	<dw_control_name>.SaveAs(<filename>,<savastype>,<colheading>)	Saves the contents of the DataWindow to a file in the specified format with or without column headings at the beginning
ScrollToRow	<dw_control_name>.ScrollToRow(<row>)	Scrolls the DataWindow to the specified row. This changes the current row but not the current column
SelectRow	<dw_control_name>.SelectRow(<row>,<action>)	Highlights or cancels the highlight for the specified row in the DataWindow
SetItem	<dw_control_name>.SetItem(<row>,<column>,<value>)	Assigns a value to the specified cell in the DataWindow
SetText	<dw_control_name>.SetText(<string>)	Places text in the edit box that is in front of the current cell in the DataWindow
Update	<dw_control_name>.Update()	Sends to the database all inserts, changes, and deletions that the user has made in the DataWindow since the last Update function

DATAWINDOW CONTROL EVENTS

Events are activated when a DataWindow Control executes the application. Some of the DataWindow control events are listed in the chart below:

DataWindow Control Events

Event	Result
Clicked	When the user clicks a protected cell in the DataWindow or the first time you click into an unprotected cell
Constructor	Immediately before the Open event occurs in the window
DBError	When a database error occurs in the DataWindow
Destructor	Immediately after the Close event occurs in the window
Double-clicked	When the user double-clicks a noneditable field or between fields in the DataWindow
DragDrop	When a dragged control is dropped on the DataWindow control
DragEnter	When a dragged control enters the DataWindow control
DragLeave	When a dragged control leaves the DataWindow control
DragWithin	When a dragged control is within the DataWindow control
EditChanged	When a user types in an edit control in the DataWindow
GetFocus	Just before the DataWindow control receives focus
ItemChanged	When the user modifies a field and presses Enter or changes focus
ItemError	When a field is modified, the field loses focus, and a value does not pass the input validation rule defined in the Database painter or DataWindow painter for that column
ItemFocusChanged	When the current item in the control changes
LoseFocus	When the DataWindow control loses focus
Other	A Windows message other than a PowerBuilder event
PrintEnd	The printing of the DataWindow ends
PrintPage	Before each page of the DataWindow is formatted for printing
PrintStart	When the printing of the DataWindow starts
RButtonDown	When the right mouse button is pressed in unoccupied area of the window
Resize	When the user or a script resizes a DataWindow control
RetrieveEnd	When the retrieval of the DataWindow is complete
RetrieveRow	After a row has been retrieved
RetrieveStart	When the retrieval for the DataWindow is about to begin
RowFocusChanged	When the current row changes in the DataWindow
ScrollHorizontal	When the user scrolls right or left in the DataWindow control with the TAB or arrow keys or the scroll bar

Event	Result
ScrollVertical	The user scrolls up or down in the DataWindow control with the TAB or arrow keys or the scroll bar
SQLPreview	After a Retrieve, Update, or ReselectRow function call and immediately before the SQL statement is submitted to the DBMS
UpdateEnd	When all the updates from the DataWindow to the database are complete
UpdateStart	After an update function call and just before changes in the DataWindow are sent to the database

13

Creating a PowerBuilder Executable

To deliver an executable version of your application, you create an .exe file. After completing this chapter, you will be able to create this file using three methods.

Whenever you save an object, such as a window or menu, in a painter, PowerBuilder saves the object in a library (a .pbl file). After completing this chapter, you will understand how to use the PowerBuilder Library painter, and how to create an executable with multiple .pbl's.

THE LIBRARY PAINTER

The Library painter is used to organize and maintain libraries and the entries in each library, and to organize access to entries.

From the Library painter, you can:

- Browse through library entries
- Build a dynamic runtime library (.pbd)
- Check out or check in entries
- Copy and move library entries to another library
- Create a new library on the current drive or another drive
- Delete any library entries or libraries that are no longer needed

- Display and manipulate the entries in a library
- Export library entries to ASCII files so that you can move application source programs or keep track of changes to the source programs during development
- Import library entries from these exported ASCII files
- List checked-out entries
- Print reports on you application and any of its objects
- Regenerate compiled object definitions from source files

Accessing the Library Painter

To access the Library painter, select the Library icon from the PowerPanel or the PowerBar:

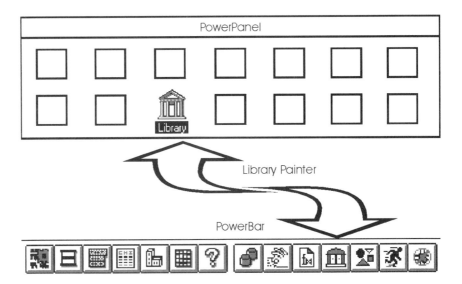

Libraries and directories that contain libraries on the current drive display in file folder icons when the Library painter is opened. Across the top you will see other drives available.

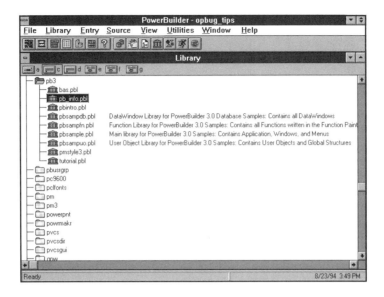

Expanding a Directory

Double-click the file folder icon to expand the directory.

Double-click on the name of a PowerBuilder Library (.pbl) to select it.

Double-click on the name again to close the entry.

Library Entries

For all entries:

- The current directory is the directory that contains the most recent library used in PowerBuilder
- The file extension .pbl is required when you enter a library name
- When the directory is on a drive other than the current drive, select the drive and then select the directory
- To select multiple entries, hold down the ctrl key and click the entries you want to select, or click on an entry, then, holding the shift key down, click on another entry to select entries in between
- Click the Select All button on the toolbar or select Select All from the Library menu to select all the entries in a library

CREATING A LIBRARY

To create a new library:

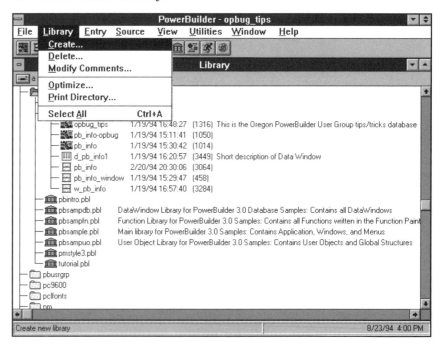

1. From the Library menu select Create. The Create Library window is presented with the name of the current directory and a list of the libraries and subdirectories in the current directory.

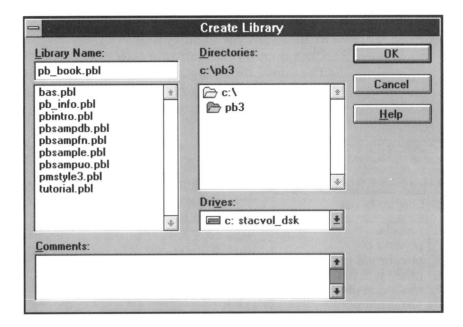

2. In the Library Name box, type the name of the library you want to create.
3. Decide which directory: either accept the current directory or choose the parent directory from the list.
4. Type in additional comments if needed.
5. Click OK. Your library will be created by PowerBuilder.

Note: If you make a mistake you can delete the library by selecting Delete from the library menu. A library cannot be renamed in the Library painter.

MANIPULATING LIBRARY ENTRIES

Library entries can be manipulated in a number of ways.

Copying

Before you copy entries to a library, the library must be in the library search path of the current application. To copy a library entry from one library to another library:

1. From the Library painter directory tree, select the library entries that you want to copy.
2. Click Copy on the toolbar or select Copy from the Entry menu. The Copy Library Entries window is presented with the name of the current directory and a list of libraries and subdirectories in the current directory.

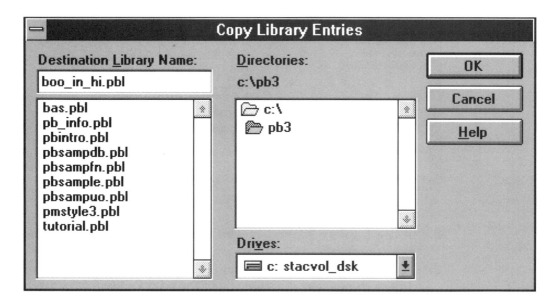

3. Select or type in the destination library.

   To copy entries to a library in the current directory, select the library from the listbox under the Destination Library Name box.

   To copy entries to a library in another directory, use either of these methods:

- Using the Drives and Directories boxes, select the destination directory. Then select the library from the list or enter the library name in the Destination Library Name box.
- Enter the fully qualified name of the library in the Destination Library Name box.

4. Click OK.

Browsing

You can browse library entries to identify those that contain a specific search string, object attributes, scripts, and/or variables. Also, you can select the types of information that the Library painter will present for each object in which it finds the search string. To initiate a Browse search:

1. Select one or more library entries.
2. From the Entry menu select Browse Entries or click Browse on the toolbar. The Browse Library Entries window is presented.

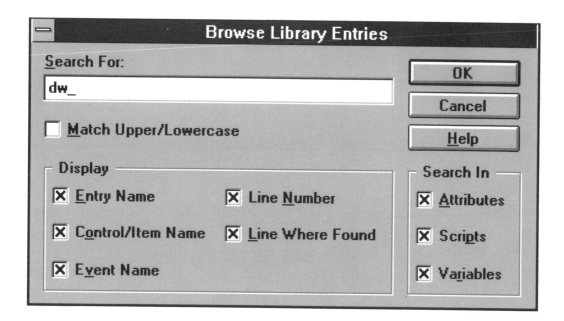

3. In the Search For box, enter a string.
4. To restrict the search to comparing the case of the characters, click the Match Upper/Lowercase box.
5. For each object that contains the search string, select the types of information you want to see.
6. Select the components of each object that you want Browse to inspect: Attributes, Scripts, and Variables.
7. Click OK.

Matching Library Entries Window When Browse finds one or more objects that contain the search string, it lists them in a Matching Library Entries window.

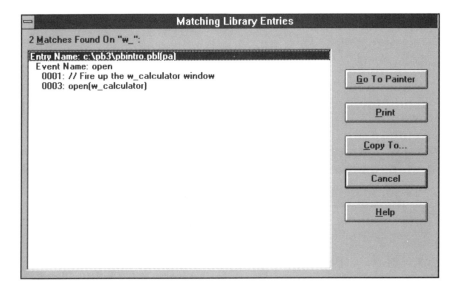

Select an entry and click the Go To Painter button to activate the PowerBuilder painter for that object.

Print the list of matching entries by clicking the Print button.

Copy the list of matching entries to an ASCII file by clicking the Copy To button.

Moving

A library entry can be moved from its current library to another library in the same directory or in another directory. Power-Builder automatically stores the entry in its new library and deletes it from its old library.

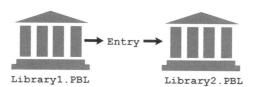

Library1.PBL → Entry → Library2.PBL

To move a library entry:

1. Select the library entries in the Library painter directory tree.
2. Select Move from the Entry menu or click the Move button on the toolbar. The Move Library Entries window is presented with the name of the current directory and a list of libraries and subdirectories in the current directory.
3. Select or type in the destination library.
4. Click OK.

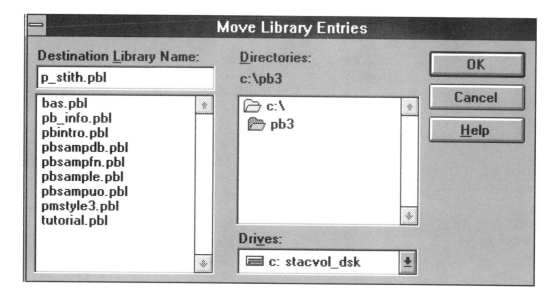

Deleting

1. From the Library painter directory tree, select the library entries you want to delete.
2. From the Entry menu select Delete or click Delete from the toolbar. A message box will be presented to verify the deletion.

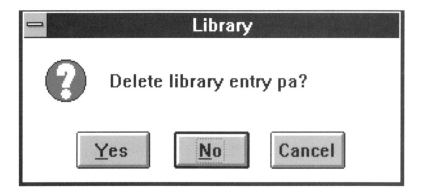

- Click Yes to delete the entry.
- Click No to cancel the deletion of the current entry only; you can continue to delete the selected entries that have not been deleted.
- Click Cancel to cancel the deletion of the current entry and all subsequent selected entries.

Note: Once a library entry has been deleted, it cannot be restored.

Regenerating

When a new version of PowerBuilder is released or when an ancestor object is changed, you may need to regenerate library entries. PowerBuilder uses the source to regenerate the library entry and replaces the current compiled object with the regenerated object.

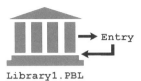

Library1.PBL

To regenerate a library entry:

1. From the list displayed in the Library Painter directory tree, select the library entry.
2. From the Entry menu select Regenerate or click Regenerate on the toolbar.

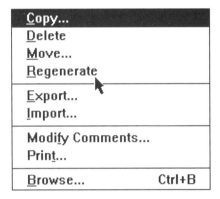

Note: When you import a library entry, PowerBuilder regenerates it and creates the new object.

EXPORTING AND IMPORTING LIBRARY ENTRIES

Exporting

One or more library entries can be exported to external disk files. This is useful when you want to convert library entries to an ASCII file format so that you can use a source library management system to control and track changes to the PowerBuilder source during development.

Library1.PBL

An exported file contains PowerScript source code that fully defines the associated PowerBuilder object, including its attributes and PowerScript routines that you developed for its events.

Note: The purpose of the export features is to export source programs, not to modify the source programs. It is recommended that you do not modify source programs in an ASCII file.

To Convert a Library Entry to ASCII File Format

1. From the list displayed in the Library painter workspace, select the entries to convert.
2. From the Entry menu select Export or click the Export button on the toolbar. The Export Library Entries window is presented with the name of the first entry selected for export in the File Name box and the name of the current directory beside it.

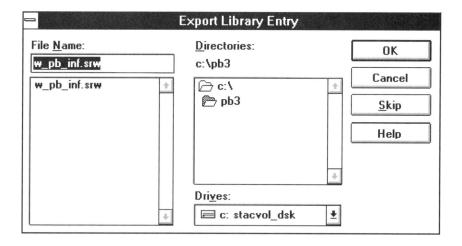

3. Select the destination directory or accept the default directory.
4. Click OK. PowerBuilder will:
   - Convert the entry to ASCII file format
   - Store it with an export name in the destination directory
   - Display the next entry you selected for export

   When a file already exists with the default export filename, a prompt displays to verify that you want to replace it.
   - Click Yes to replace the entry
   - Click No to change the entry name. The Export Library Entries window is presented with the name of the file. Change the export filename and then export the file, skip the file, or cancel the export of the current file and all selected files that have not been exported.
5. Repeat steps 1-4 until all entries have been processed. Click Skip to skip an entry. Click Cancel to exit the Export Library Entries window before all the entries have been exported or skipped.

The following screen print displays a portion of the contents of an exported file:

```
┌─────────────────────────────────────────────────────────────┐
│ ▭         DOS File Editor - W_PB_INF.SRW              ▼ ▲ │
├─────────────────────────────────────────────────────────────┤
│ $PBExportHeader$w_pb_info.srw                              ▲│
│ forward                                                     ┃│
│ global type w_pb_info from Window                           ┃│
│ end type                                                    ┃│
│ type st_1 from statictext within w_pb_info                  ┃│
│ end type                                                    ┃│
│ type sle_1 from singlelineedit within w_pb_info             ┃│
│ end type                                                    ┃│
│ type dw_1 from datawindow within w_pb_info                  ┃│
│ end type                                                    ┃│
│ type cb_close from commandbutton within w_pb_info           ┃│
│ end type                                                    ┃│
│ end forward                                                 ┃│
│                                                             ┃│
│ global type w_pb_info from Window                           ┃│
│ int X=51                                                    ┃│
│ int Y=25                                                    ▼│
│ ◄ ▮                                                    ►    │
│                                                   0001:0001 │
└─────────────────────────────────────────────────────────────┘
```

Importing

In PowerBuilder you can convert a library entry from exported ASCII file format to PowerBuilder format and regenerates the object from source.

Library1.PBL

Note: The library must be in the library search path of the current application before you can import entries to a library.

To import a library entry:

1. From the Entry menu select Import or click Import on the toolbar. The Import File into Library Entry window is presented with the name of the current directory and a list of files with the extension .sr*.

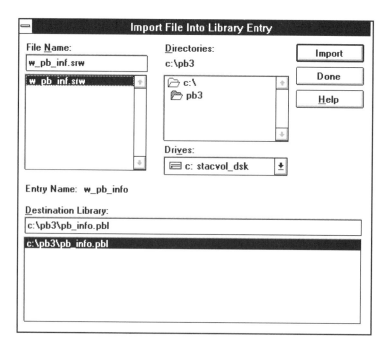

2. In the File Name Box, select the file from the list or type the name of the file you are importing for the source file.
   - To import the entry to a library in the *current* directory, select the library from the list or enter the name of the library in the Destination Library Name box.
   - To import the entry from a library in *another* directory:
     - Select the destination directory using the Drives and Directories boxes, then select the library from the list or enter the library name in the Destination Library Name box.
     - Enter the fully qualified name of the library in the Destination Library Name box.
3. Click Import. PowerBuilder will:
   - Convert the specified library entry to PowerBuilder format
   - Regenerate the object
   - Store the entry in the specified library

Note: If a library entry with the same name already exists in the selected library, PowerBuilder will replace it with the imported entry.

4. Type in the name of the next ASCII file to import or click Done to return to the Library painter workspace.

Optimizing

PowerBuilder libraries should be optimized on a regular basis. As you change and maintain windows, menus, DataWindows, and functions, the objects get bigger and their places in the library can change. This can cause areas of unused space within the library. Optimizing the library removes these unused areas. To optimize a library:

1. Open the Library painter. From the Library menu select Optimize:
2. Select the library to be optimized.
3. Click OK.

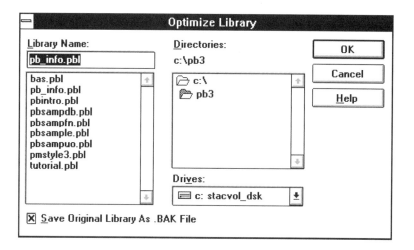

PRINTING APPLICATION REPORTS

You can use the print feature to document the objects you have created in your application during development. These reports can be specific in information you want printed. PowerBuilder generates the selected reports and sends them to the printer specified in Printer Setup in the File menu. To create library entry reports:

1. Select one or more library entries.
2. Select print from the Entry menu.

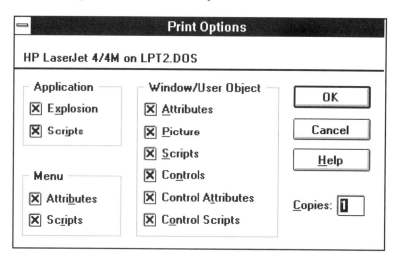

THE POWERBUILDER EXECUTABLE

The PowerBuilder Executable (.exe) is the file that is delivered to the users so that they may execute the finished application outside the PowerBuilder development environment. The PowerBuilder .exe file contains the following:

PowerBuilder runtime bootstrap routine

The application icon (optional)

The compiled code for each object in the application

TECHNIQUES FOR CREATING THE EXECUTABLE

There are three techniques in creating executables.

Technique 1: Building an Executable in a Single File The first technique allows the developer to store the application in one .exe file. This is the preferred method for small applications, as it allows the developer to deliver a single file to the user.

Technique 2: Building an Executable and Application Libraries The second technique allows the developer to break the application into logical pieces. This is particularly helpful for the development and maintenance in large applications. If a revision or update is made to a particular piece of the application, the only part that has to be moved to production is the effected .pbd (dynamic runtime library). (See Structure on page 276.)

Technique 3: A Combination of Techniques 1 and 2 The third technique is a combination of the first two techniques. The .exe contains the compiled code of one or more .pbl's containing mission critical functions. The rest of the application is in the .pbd's. The structure looks the same as Technique 2.

Technique 1: A Single Executable File

Structure:

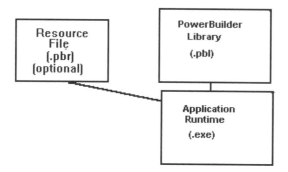

Techniques 2 and 3: Executables and .pbd's

Structure:

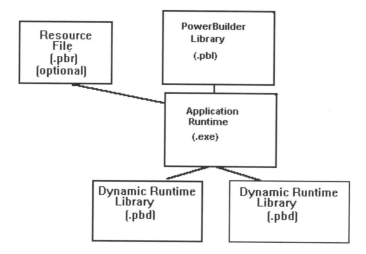

STEPS IN CREATING THE EXECUTABLE

Building an Application Executable

Optimize the application library or libraries (.pbl) in the Library painter.

Create a dynamic runtime library for each .pbl in the Library painter. This procedure is only applicable for techniques 2 and 3.

Select Libraries in the Application painter and make sure all the libraries (.pbl's) for the application are included in the search path.

From the Application painter, build the Runtime file.

Optimizing PowerBuilder Code

All PowerBuilder .pbl's should be optimized before an executable or library is built. Optimization will allow the PowerBuilder code to run faster and more efficiently.

Select the Library painter from the PowerBuilder Power Panel.

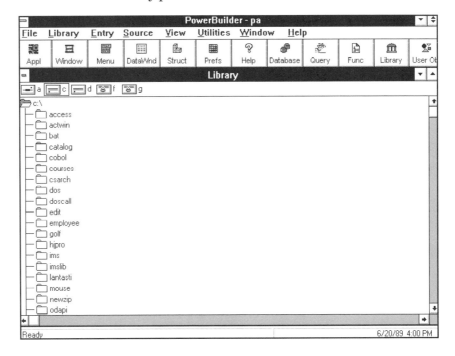

Optimize Library Window

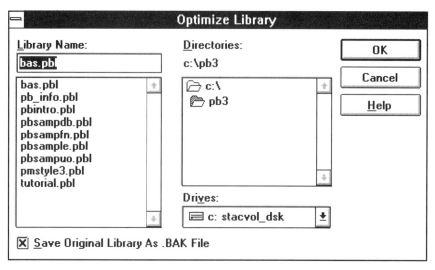

Click on the .pbl name in the Library tree to optimize the .pbl.

Choose Optimize Library in the Library menu selection.

Select the Save Original Library as .bak File checkbox, if you chose to backup the file before the optimization.

Repeat optimization for all affected libraries.

Select Application Window

Select the Applications painter icon, then the Open button, and the Select Application window will open:

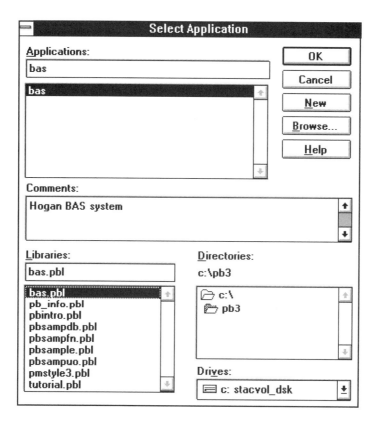

Select the application for which runtime is being created
Select the OK pushbutton

Select Libraries Window

Select the LibList pushbutton from the PainterBar and the Select Libraries window will open.

Verify that all the libraries that are needed for the application executable are included in the Library Search Path.

If all the libraries are not present, select the appropriate libraries from the Paste Libraries window by double-clicking on the library to add.

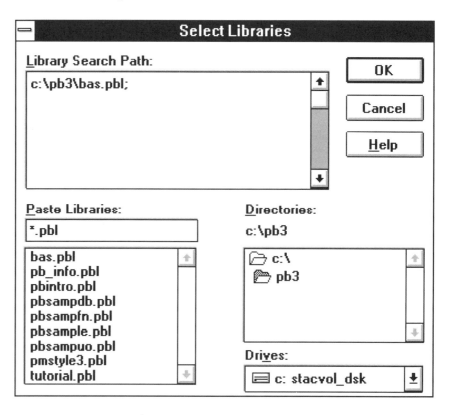

If the libraries needed are not on the drive and directory in the Drives and Directory windows, select the appropriate drive and directory.

Click the OK pushbutton when complete.

Creating the Executable

Technique 1 for Creating the .exe Select the Create Executable pushbutton from the Painter Bar.

Create Executable window:

```
┌─────────────────────────────────────────────────────────┐
│ ═                    Create Executable                    │
├─────────────────────────────────────────────────────────┤
│ Executable Name:        Directories:         ┌─────────┐  │
│ ┌──────────────────┐    c:\pb3               │   OK    │  │
│ │bas.exe           │                         └─────────┘  │
│ └──────────────────┘    ┌──────────────┐     ┌─────────┐  │
│ ┌──────────────┐ ▲      │ 🗁 c:\      ▲ │     │ Cancel  │  │
│ │db32w.exe     │ ┃      │ 🗀 pb3       │ │     └─────────┘  │
│ │dbbackw.exe   │ ┃      │              │ │     ┌─────────┐  │
│ │dberasew.exe  │ ┃      │              │ │     │  Help   │  │
│ │dbexpanw.exe  │ ┃      │              │ │     └─────────┘  │
│ │dbinitw.exe   │ ┃      │              │ │                  │
│ │dblogw.exe    │ ┃      │              │ │                  │
│ │dbshrinw.exe  │ ┃      │            ▼ │ │                  │
│ │dbstartw.exe  │ ┃      └──────────────┘ │                  │
│ │dbtranw.exe   │ ┃      Drives:          │                  │
│ │dbunloaw.exe  │ ┃      ┌──────────────┐ │                  │
│ │dbvalidw.exe  │ ┃      │ 💾 c: stacvol_dsk ▼ │            │
│ │dbwritew.exe  │ ▼      └──────────────┘ │                  │
│ └──────────────┘                          │                  │
│ Dynamic Libraries:                                          │
│ ┌─────────────────────────────────────────────────────┐  │
│ │c:\pb3\bas.pbl                                          │  │
│ │                                                        │  │
│ │                                                        │  │
│ │                                                        │  │
│ └─────────────────────────────────────────────────────┘  │
│ Additional Resources File Name:                            │
│ ┌─────────────────────────────────────────────┐  ┌──────┐ │
│ │                                               │  │ Files│ │
└─────────────────────────────────────────────────────────┘
```

Note the Dynamic Libraries window reflects the libraries in the Library Search Path window

Change the Drives and/or Directory window if needed

If the application requires a resource file (.pbr), then click on the Files pushbutton and select the application resource file (.pbr), then click the OK pushbutton. See chapter 3 for a discussion of resource files.

Click on the OK pushbutton to create the executable. This will create a .exe which contains the complete application

In the example above, a bas.exe file would be created that contains all the compiled objects and definitions of bas.pbl

Technique 2 Using this method, the user creates the dynamic runtime file (.pbd) for each of the .pbl's in the Library painter, after each of the .pbl's have been optimized.

Select Build Dynamic Library from the menu labeled Utilities in the Library painter and open the Build Dynamic Runtime Library window:

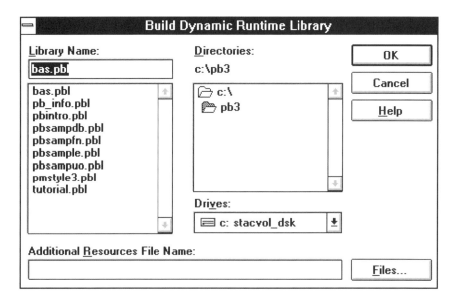

Select the .pbl from the Library painter tree and choose Build Dynamic Runtime Library from the Utilities pulldown menu.

Select PowerBuilder Resource Files, if needed, using the Files pushbutton to select a file. File name will appear in the Additional Resources File Name box.

Create Executable window:

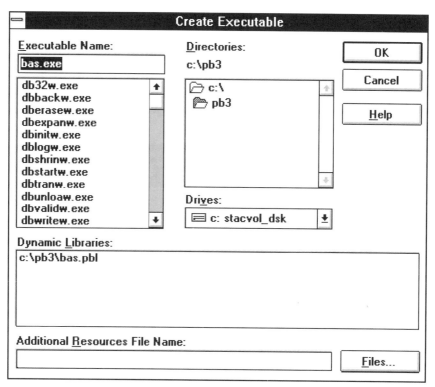

Notice the difference from technique 1: All the .pbl's are listed in the Dynamic Libraries window. These .pbl's will be referenced, but not included, in the executable. Click the OK pushbutton and this will create a .exe that acts as a driver for all of the selected .pbd's.

Note the Dynamic Libraries window reflects the libraries in the Library Search Path window.

If the application requires a resource file (.pbr), then click on the Files pushbutton and select the application resource file (.pbr). See chapter 3 for a discussion of resource files.

In the example above bas.exe would be the driver for the application; it will not contain any of the application compiled objects or definitions. The application definitions would be contained in the application Dynamic Runtime Libraries, bas.pbl.

The benefit of this technique would be realized in the situation where the executable and all the .pbd's had been distributed to the customer, and later, one of the .pbl's requires maintenance. The only step required after the maintenance is completed would be to distribute the new .pbd: Just optimize the library, build the Dynamic Runtime Library, and redistribute to the customer.

Technique 3 Method three involves a combination of the first two techniques.

Create Executable window:

Create the .pbd's for the libraries you want to remain as .pbd's in the Library painter as in technique 2.

Creating the .exe, highlight the .pbl's in the Dynamic Libraries window to be used as .pbd's. The unhighlighted .pbl's will become part of the .exe.

In the example above, bas.pbl's compiled objects and definitions will be in the bas.exe, and any other .pbl's and any unhighlighted .pbl's will be .pbd's not contained in the .exe.

14

PowerBuilder Tips and Techniques

After completing this chapter, you will be able to understand some of the potential pitfalls to avoid in the PowerBuilder development environment. We will discuss the size of a .pbl. We will also discuss optimizing a .pbl, what it does, and how it can help.

In addition, we will discuss some shortcut keys, and how to provide online help in your application.

A FEW POWERBUILDER TIPS

The Size of a .pbl .pbl's should not be allowed to grow larger than 800K. The PowerBuilder documentation notes that if a .pbl becomes larger than 800K, some unpredictable results may occur.

Optimize, Optimize, Optimize .pbl's should be optimized often. Optimizing a .pbl removes old or logically deleted code and brings the .pbl back to a reasonable size. If your application begins to react unpredictably (i.e., code that used to work all of a sudden doesn't), the first thing you should try is optimization. This will often solve your problem.

For OOD: Regenerate, Regenerate, Regenerate If you are using PowerBuilder to do object-oriented development (i.e., inheriting objects from base classes, etc.) you will also run into unexpected results from time to time. Keep in mind that by changing a base class, you can adversely affect related objects. If you know you are changing an object that has ancestors, make sure you regenerate the ancestors and rebuild the .pbl. If you begin to get unexplainable results, look at this first.

Listbox Population: Inline SQL versus DataWindow When populating a listbox or dropdown listbox, you will achieve much faster results if you use a DataWindow to retrieve the required data as opposed to performing inline SQL (Declare, Open Cursor, Fetch). The DataWindow control is significantly faster and can often produce dramatically better results than inline SQL.

Global Variable Usage—Think about It! Try to limit the number and size of global variables your application requires. Global variables are very expensive resources.

DBMS Limitations and a Workaround Some DBMSs do not currently support UPDATE or DELETE WHERE CURRENT OF CURSOR (i.e., update or delete the record currently pointed to by the cursor). To get around this problem, create a second transaction object and use it to go against the table at the same time. Use the first transaction object to inquire; use the second to UPDATE or DELETE.

Commit! If your application is performing a large quantity of Insert, Update, and/or Delete transactions against your DBMS, make every attempt to use COMMIT or ROLLBACK as appropriate as soon as practically possible. Prior to a commit or rollback, all transaction information is stored in buffers. As these buffers become full, database performance degrades until the database actually crashes from lack of available memory to extend these buffers. A COMMIT will make all row modifications permanent and flush these buffers; a ROLL-

BACK will simply flush these buffers (without making your changes permanent).

The Hidden DataWindow A common practice of many developers is to use a DataWindow for database access without using the DataWindow for display or data entry. This method involves making the DataWindow a hidden control. In the Window painter, place the DataWindow control on the screen in a spot which will be unused by the rest of the application. Make the actual size of the DataWindow small and make the control INVISIBLE, ENABLED, with a BORDER. The DataWindow will perform the data access and then you can load or unload data from the DataWindow to the controls placed on the screen.

The Stored Procedure Executing SQL through a stored procedure is almost always more efficient and gives better performance than inline SQL. The procedure is, in fact, executed on the Database Server using its resources instead of local resources to run the query.

To DDE or Not to DDE PowerSoft will admit that its implementation of DDE is not the best. In fact, PowerBuilder DDE requires that at least 40 percent of Window's resources be available to make a connection. In other words, if you attempt to go DDE to another application (particular applications that require large quantities of resources such as Word for Windows, Excel, PowerPoint, etc). If it does work, you will find DDE to be relatively slow. One alternative is to write DDE access routines in C and call them using PowerBuilder. Another solution is to avoid DDE altogether and find another way (i.e., a flat file and a Word macro, as it turns out, works great).

SHORTCUT KEYS

The following shortcut keys can be used from anywhere within PowerBuilder to open a painter or tool.

Shortcut Keys

To Open	Press
Application Painter	shift+f1
Window Painter	shift+f2
Menu Painter	shift+f3
DataWindow Painter	shift+f4
Structure Editor	shift+f5
DOS File Editor	shift+f6
Database Painter	shift+f7
Query Painter	shift+f8
Function Painter	shift+f9
Library Painter	shift+f10

PROVIDING ONLINE HELP FOR YOUR APPLICATION

Providing online Help for your Microsoft Windows 3.x applications is a simple four-step process:

1. Create the Help text file following the directions specified in the Microsoft Windows Software Developer's Kit (SDK).
2. Create a project file (in *.hpj format) that contains the file header information the Windows 3.x Help compiler requires.
3. Compile the project (*.hpj) file into a *.hlp format file.
4. Use the PowerScript ShowHelp function to access and display the *.hlp file in you application.

Context-Sensitive Help

While in the PowerScript painter, you can get online, context-sensitive help by performing the following two-step process:

1. Place you cursor within any script statement you require Help information on.
2. Press Shift+F1.

Shortcut to Test an Object

When you are working with an object such as a Menu, a Window, or a Data Window, you can test the execution of the object by pressing the shortcut key combination of ctrl+W.

FILE NAMING CONVENTIONS

It is best to develop, and to adhere to, a consistent naming convention for all of the PowerBuilder objects that you will be creating. The following is recommended as a starting point.

File Naming Conventions

Object Type	Prefix	Object Type	Prefix
CheckBox	cbx_	Picture	p_
CommandButton	cb_	PictureButton	pb_
DataWindow	dw_	RadioButton	rb_
DropDownListBox	ddlb_	Rectangle	r_
EditMask	em_	RoundRectangle	rr_
Graph	g_	SingleLineEdit	sle_
GroupBox	gb_	StaticText	st_
HScrollBar	hsb_	VScrollBar	vsb_
Line	ln_	Query	q_
ListBox	lb_	User Objects	uo_
MultiLineEdit	mle_	Functions	f_
Oval	oval_	Window	w_

GETTING THAT 3D LOOK

Applications today routinely have a three-dimensional look to SingleLineEdit boxes. To acquire a 3D look to the SingleLineEdit boxes in your application:

1. Select Default To 3D from the Options menu.

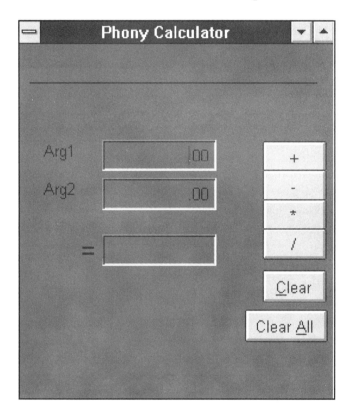

This will automatically set the window background color to gray and uses 3D borders when you position controls.

About the Author

Jim Hobuss is President of HCS, Inc., a high-technology company specializing in MIS platform migration training and consulting. HCS, Inc. offices are located in Portland, Ore., Hartford, Conn., and Toronto, Canada. The author is a frequent speaker at various industry association meetings, the author of numerous trade magazine articles, and generally recognized as the father of application development centers and the successful implementation of new technologies in programming departments. He is the Editor and Publisher of the *Workbench Focus* newsletter, a quarterly publication targeted to PC workstation programmers and analysts. He holds a Bachelor of Science degree from Portland State University.

Jim can be contacted at:

HCS Inc.
18004 SE Marie Street
Portland, OR 97236-1338
(503) 661-3421
(503) 661-2477 fax
76507,2120 CompuServe Id
JHOBUSS@Netcom.com (Internet address)

Index